D0461948

Here's Your CHANCE

Written by Christina Dalpiaz

Edited by Yash Holbrook

Illustrated by C. A. McCall

&

Inspired by Katlin

Here's Your CHANCE
Changing How Adults Nurture Children's Egos

1995 Printing

Copyright © 1995 By Christina Dalpiaz
All Rights Reserved

Library of Congress Cataloging-in-Publication Data
Dalpiaz, Christina M.

ISBN 0-9650669-0-8

Published in the United States

PRINTED IN THE UNITED STATES OF AMERICA

Contents

Foreword

I decided to write this book because of my love for my nephew, Katlin. My nephew's courage and tenacity have shown me that as long as parents are willing to protect and nurture their children, they will stand tall and strive for the highest.

I have other nieces and nephews that deserve mentioning. Thank you, Charlie, Michael, Paige, Willie, Chris, Michelle and Reed for being my inspiration. You all mean so much to me.

I would also like to thank Yash Holbrook for his compassion, technical expertise and editing skills. I could not have made it through this book without him.

Introduction

Much of what I've written are insights from my own experiences as an observer. For more than eleven years I taught parenting techniques to improve interactive skills between parents and children. I worked with children in domestic violence shelters, with abused teenagers and with new parents just looking for support. With all of this experience, I truly believed that I had the *insight.*

The revelation that maybe I didn't know everything came about three years ago when I became a para-parent to my nephew, Katlin. Being a parent is much more overwhelming than I could have ever imagined. My expectations for other parents now seemed unrealistic. I always believed that parents could be *in control* of their children at all times if they would only tried harder. Now I realize that anyone who must actually live with a child on a 24-hour basis will sooner or later—lose a grip. Learning to manage these times is the main objective of this book.

As I began having parenting problems, I took my own advice (after all, I considered myself the "expert"). Many times the advice worked (what else should I expect from an "expert?"). But to my amazement, there were times when my advice didn't work (now I'm talking reality check).

When I "failed," I felt befuddled. There were times where I would stop writing this book because I felt I was failing as a parent. What right did I have to give advice. Then it hit me—I realized that making mistakes were not necessarily failures—just opportunities to start over. This revelation would help me realize the frame of mind I needed to work with my nephew and help nurture him through his childhood.

My nephew was placed in my care due to unfortunate personal circumstances. His life was turned up-side down. I saw an angry disassociated child who was incapable of love. As I worked with him and would share my techniques with others, they would say, *"Wow, you should write a book."* So I started writing and writing and here I am two and a half years later.

What I've learned through this challenging experience, I would like to share with others and hopefully help parents who might be experiencing some of the same difficulties.

As you read through these chapters, understand that everyone's experiences are different; and although I feel much of what I am saying is good, there may be things we disagree on. We all live in our own reality and no one is wrong or right—just different—that's what makes life so exciting.

I would like to add that although I'm aware of most of my mistakes, I'm sure I will continue making and perhaps even repeating mistakes as long as I am a parent. I must consciously practice parenting each and every day. Although, I have a degree in psychology, a credential in early childhood development, a certification in victims' advocacy and I am the director of child advocate group called CHANCE (Changing How Adults Nurture Children's Egos), I must continuously try to be a better parent.

Despite my knowledge, I sometimes slip back into old habits and must struggle to get back on the right track.

Some parents buy books like *Here's Your CHANCE* expecting to find all the answers. We do not live in a perfect world where everyone is the same and there are never any problems. We cannot possibly be perfect parents and no one book will solve all your needs—but it can't hurt. I hope you find this book as enlightening and entertaining as it was for me to write it. Good luck and good parenting.

How to Read This Book

Any information contained in this book is subject to each reader's interpretation and opinion. Everyone's opinion is their own and should be valued and trusted by its owner—that's what makes life so exciting and challenging.

In researching for this book, I found that consistency was probably the most difficult problem that most parents faced yet, at the same time, the most essential to parenting. To use the techniques in this book, it would be to your benefit to read the book slowly and concentrate on each chapter. If you are having problems initially with changing behavior, be patient and don't get discouraged—it will come. Changing behaviors is essentially changing old habits—and old habits die hard. Repetition is the only way to see results. So practice...practice...practice...

I've learned that becoming a parent automatically makes people prone to mistakes, irritability, and disorientation. It's an extremely tough job that requires 24 hour maintenance...we're bound to mess up. When we can accept this fact, we will be able to see failure as just another opportunity to start over. Making mistakes is the reality—if you accept that then your battle is half won. Awareness is a critical factor in changing behavior—the rest is practice.

If there is anything that I would like to stress the most, it's that we need to remember that tomorrow is always a new day and that we have the CHANCE to begin again. Learning from our mistakes rather than repeating them is one of the best things we can do for our children. I like to take each new day and make new resolutions. It beats waiting for New Year's.

Each chapter contains a least one homework assignment and a journal page. It would be beneficial to read each chapter then work on the assignment. This will help reinforce what you have read. I would recommend practicing the new techniques before moving onto the next chapter. Good luck and have fun!

CHAPTER ONE

I AM THE POTTER,
YOU ARE MY CLAY

I Am The Potter, You Are My Clay

Molding Your Children

There are many different approaches to raising children—some better and some worse than others. And there really isn't any single right way to approach it. Parenting skills develop as you learn about your child. Fortunately, there are resources available to help you choose methods that might work for your situation. This book is one such resource that will provide new ideas and strategies to help you improve some of your current techniques, adopt new ones or discard ineffective ones.

Although there are no strategies that guarantee success, one thing is certain: We can and must do our best. And no matter what, we must keep trying. When we recognize that something isn't working, it's our responsibility as the care giver to try a different approach—always being guided by the importance of keeping what works and throwing out what doesn't. We need to be aware of the parenting tools we are using so that we get the job done *right*.

It's natural for us to want the very best for our children and often we'll get discouraged when things don't run so smoothly as we would like. The trouble is—we're striving for perfection—which is not only unrealistic, but unhealthy. We have the lives of these children in the palms of our hands. With each turn of the potter's wheel, we are molding and shaping their future person.

"Don't Should On Yourself"

When you get caught up in all the *shoulds* and *should nots* in life, you limit a child's potential along with your own. For each time you practice the *shoulds*, you create an environment that promotes quitting.

Save your *shoulds* for when it counts. For instance, you *should* be kind to people and you *should not* steal or kill someone. If you *should* too much, your child will begin to tune out what you are trying to teach him and he will only hear the negative which lies within your message. The goal of parenting is to get your children to understand what life is all about and to help them learn what it means to be able to get along in the world. Growing up can be so complicated and painful for anyone but especially for the children of this generation. They need positive guidance to make it through this transitional time.

Lighten up and consider whether what you're *shoulding* is really so important. Perhaps it would be a good exercise to assess whether you are placing these same limitations on yourself. Then decide whether your *should* will make you or your child the person you or she really needs to be? If not—stop *shoulding* on yourself and the ones you love.

The Core of the Inner Child

A child's basic need is to be loved and cared for. This need doesn't go away simply because she grows up. No matter how old she is, the need to be nurtured and loved will still be there. That's why we develop friendships, get married and have children. A person's ego continuously requires nourishment from others. There exists in all of us an inner child—we are really only children living in grown up bodies.

Needs change in degree as we grow. But, we mustn't deny their existence. Nor can we deny that our children possess these same basic needs. Remember how it felt to be a child and hopefully that will aid in the quest to sculpt the lives of your children.

Practicing awareness will make this molding process somewhat easier. Keep in mind; though, that your children are not you. As much as you might desire sameness...you must let your children be their *own* person. While sculpting them, also keep in mind that they aren't always going to be receptive to the same forms of disciplines and motivations that 'seemed' to worked on you as a child. So, be creative. Think beyond who you were and are and the sky will be the limit. Your children have experienced different ideas and different concepts that go beyond your realm. You'll need to change your approach and appreciate them in order to successfully deal with their differences.

A single set of rules cannot be applied to all children. The methods your parents used with you might not necessarily work for them. You'll need to use your imagination to conquer new and different parenting issues if you want to see results.

Because you live with your children day-in and day-out, no one else understands their qualities better than you do. Use this to your advantage—it's never too late. Whether or not you've made mistakes in the past, you can make up for them now—just throw away those parenting techniques that don't work and begin anew.

Mistakes and failures are just opportunities to start over. Mistakes encourage growth. Everything and everybody has room for that. *Here's your CHANCE* to be creative, innovative and challenged! What more could a parent want?

Although children have differences, they also share many similarities. For example, I've never met a child who didn't experience the "terrible twos." Nor have I met one that didn't interrupt his parents when they were on the telephone. There is a familiar developmental sequence that all children take so a list of similarities can be created as a baseline. Make a list that pertains to you and establish criteria based on these similarities and let it serve as your foundation. Once the baseline is created, varying the approaches to meet each child's circumstances will make the differences easier to deal with.

You can rely on some of your childhood experiences as a baseline also, but don't expect them all to work because your child is not you. Empathize with him and remember how it felt as a child to be dependent and vulnerable. This can enlighten and help you make better choices for your children. Your guidance is a gift to your children. Guidance and wisdom, along with consistency, will help nurture your children's ego. The thing to remember is that we can only plant and nourish the seeds. It takes the other elements of nature to supply the rest. You must take care to remember that guidance and wisdom are *always gifts*—children can either accept them or disregard them.

We must create an atmosphere of unconditional love and be a positive role model—then hope that what we've taught them will serve as a foundation for other aspects in their lives. In my opinion, role modeling is the best way to guide children. As we will learn in chapter 4, *"Hey, I'm Talking To You"*—what we do *not* say is much more important than what we do. Later in chapter 4, we will also learn how body language affects children's behavior.

"No matter where we come from, we have all lived in childhood"[1]

This is probably one of the most important aspects of all. Every parent—no matter what color, race or culture—has experienced the hardships of growing up. Remembering how it felt to be a kid can help you make better choices for them. Step back in time to an age where you felt the most vulnerable, awkward and dependent upon your parents. Use that as a reference point (everyone's situation will be different) when disciplining or relating to your children.

You need to rely on those childhood experiences to better understand where your children's ideas and thoughts are coming from. Embrace the feelings you once felt in order to appreciate the turmoil of growing. *"Childhood—Been there, done that."* If you can remember this simple thought, you will understand and deal with your children better. Most parents struggle with many of the same frustrations—parenting problems are not unique. Understanding and appreciating the fact that you are not alone can also ease your sense of isolation.

There are many different theories concerning childhood development. Some experts claim that children can be taught to be anything a parent wants them to be. Others insist that children are born with their personality and there isn't anything that can be done to influence that.

---

[1] Great Expectation, "Childhood" video tape

"Give me a child for eight years and it will be a Bolshevik forever."
-Lenin

What I hear Lenin saying is that, he can mold any child and make him exactly what he wants him to be, so long as he could expose his ideas to him for an extended period of time. This concept has some validity. Evaluate the dynamics of your family and you'll see that often your children display many of the same behavioral traits as you do. But, at the same time, remember that children are separate individuals with their own agendas. Trying to create a carbon copy of yourself won't work. If your role modeling is positive and attractive enough, your children will in all probability emulate you and your behavior. Let them accept the traits that are most appealing.

Your children will have many of your similarities—simply because of their exposure to you on a day-to-day basis. If you look hard enough, you can see a resemblance between yourself and your parents without being an exact carbon copy. A variety of experiences and exposures made you different yet your basic core is probably very similar. The scary part is—that the older you get—the more like your parents you become. **Warning this book contains facts that may be hazardous to your sanity and is not liable for any negative revelations that you may experience.

Basically, we all want what's best for our children. That's why we try to *guide* them all we can. It is my opinion that if we encourage children to be kind, respectful, responsible and loving, we've done a lot. But again we have limitations on what we can do. Think back for a moment: were there times that your parents tried to impose a particular value system upon you that you strongly disagreed with? Here's my example:

> *"Eat that liver, there are starving children in Africa that would love to have a good meal."*

The tragic fact is there are children in Africa starving but I'm not convinced that eating *that stuff* is going to change anything. Try and remember one of those particular times that impacted you the most. Now answer the following questions. Did your parents' approach work? (I never ate the liver.) Did you learn what they were trying to teach you? (I learned that I wasn't very hungry and that I should feel guilty about it.) Is it a part of your value system today? (I still can't find any really good use for liver.) Do you maintain every philosophy that your parents tried to forcibly stuff down your throat? (No, but some I do.)

Nature vs. Nurture

I believe that a child's character is developed both through the "nature" and "nurture" concept. Now, you are saying, *"Great, let's make this as complicated as possible."* Believe it or not, this is good. Having the ability to learn both inherently and environmentally is a plus because it expands your choices. Look at it this way. If you're having difficulties with your child and you see that many of his *undesirable* attributes are similar to yours or your spouse's, like the following, you have other options.

(1)   *"He is as stubborn as his father."*

(2)   *"She is narrow-minded and opinionated—just like her mother."*

This could be your CHANCE to make a choice—you can either write the child off or you can say,

> *"Okay, plan "A" will not work because plan "A" is trying to change something inherent, so I'll switch to plan "B" and find a way to influence her environmentally and see if that works."*

Believing that there is only one option will put you in a position of helplessness. In other words—you're hosed. You might as well throw up your hands and give up. But are you going to do that? Of course not. Because you love your children *unconditionally* and want to give it (parenting) all you've got...even if it kills you.

In order to help in the search for what to do for your children, you need to understand their personality and how you *respond* to it. This is very important because your reaction (or your parenting style) will either discourage or encourage your children's behavior.

Breaking the Mold

We all have experiences—some good, some not-so-good. The point being, we carry around our own spare baggage that has nothing to do with our children. We've spent a lifetime collecting this stuff and shouldn't be so anxious to pass it on to our children. Experiences that affected us as children are not necessarily going to make the same impact on our children.

An example may be that as a child, you never owned a nice pair of shoes. You felt humiliated and embarrassed. So now you refuse to let your child wear tattered shoes because you *know* it would devastate her. For her, wearing a pair of hole-y shoes is not a big deal because she didn't experience the constant humiliation that you did. Therefore, these hole-y shoes will not have the same impact as they did for you. Your child may only wear bad shoes once in her lifetime while you felt the humiliation for your entire childhood. You can attempt to protect her from the hurt but there's a good chance that the hurt is not real, it is only your *projection* of your hurt that is real.

"Listen, learn, have fun and I can do it if I try"
-Poppy Andrews[2]

Some cultures stress the importance of excelling. These cultures believe that every child is capable of learning socially, academically and spiritually. The philosophy is that if a child fails, it is a direct reflection on the teachers, the parents and the community as a whole. I see many benefits to this philosophy, yet I also see many drawbacks. Education and culture can be so highly emphasized that some children can make it while others just

---

[2] Poppy was a daycare provider that helped me tremendously through the most difficult times.

succumb to it. The pressure to succeed can be so great that children can actually suffer from stress. An example may be that Asian children, comparatively speaking, test much higher than children from the United States. The positive side to this is that these children perform better and their commitment to family is much stronger. There is something good to be said about dedication. Yet, the down side is that they will suffer more frequently from stress. We want our children to succeed and have commitment—but where do we draw the line?

We need to strike a balance. A child needs to find a place where she can learn, yet enjoy what she is learning. After all, isn't life supposed to be somewhat fun? Parents, I say to you...BALANCE...BALANCE...BALANCE...Need I say more?

You need to encourage your children to push themselves to their *own* limits—and not yours. It's important to understand that you cannot apply a single set of rules to everyone—each of us is unique. Yet no one understands a child better than his parents. You must also reassure them that every one of us has limitations and that we all need to understand where those limitations are. When you push yourself toward perfection you create an unrealistic image for your children. Letting them *falsely* believe that you are Superman and Wonderwoman is doing them a great disservice. Again I will stress—use role modeling, it works.

If you never expose your weaknesses, your kids will try to live up to those unrealistic expectations—believing that they are never quite good enough. Do kids a favor—show them that you have vulnerabilities (that you are a *real* person). Though I would encourage some caution and discretion when selecting what you tell them simply because you don't want your children to become your therapists.

What type of parent are you?

There are three types of parenting styles—authoritative, permissive and authoritarian.[3] Authoritative parents respect and genuinely like their children. They will explain limitations yet sternly follow through with love and care. Permissive parents will also like their children but they are not firm and consistent. Finally, there are authoritarian parents who are strict and often unfair. They will not regard their children with respect primarily because they just don't care. These parents believe in that saying, "Children are to be seen and not heard."

When a parent considers himself *the boss* (or should I say, the only one worthy of an opinion), he is taking the authoritarian approach to parenting and essentially it does not work. Oh sure, they might listen, but it will simply be out of fear and not because they have internalized what it was that the parent wanted to teach them. Therefore, this parent hasn't taught his children

---

[3] Helen Bee, The Developing Child, Third Edition, p. 374.

anything—only that he is bigger and stronger; and, that power wins out.

An example of the authoritarian approach is when a parent turns a child over her knee, starts spanking her and saying,

"This will teach you not to hit people who are smaller than you!"

All this parent has done is teach her that when she is an adult...she can do whatever she wants...whether it's right or wrong. If you want to be effective in teaching children these values, then learn and use negotiation skills. There are two reasons why every parent should use these skills. (1) It makes discipline more palatable and the child will more easily internalize the morals that a parent is trying to teach her. (2) If you focus on your child's positive attributes and find out what makes her tick, you will be a much more effective parent.

The next two examples are questions regarding your children's strengths and some possible solutions to improve behavior and foster a more positive and healthy development.

1. What type of temperament does the child possess? Does he respond negatively to anger or does anger get better results?

It has been my experience that most children don't work well under pressure and high degrees of tension. This can be extremely detrimental to the child who internalizes this anger and feels as though he is a bad person as a result of what he has done.

Some children will become angry and react impulsively when they are cornered and attacked...while others will just withdraw. In both cases, this is bad. You'll need to find ways to encourage your child to feel comfortable about discipline by finding ways to work around this issue. I know some of you (whether you realize it or not) are unconsciously thinking, *"I need order in my house and it's not really important to me how I get there—so long as I get there—fast."*

Order might seem important but it is not reality. Anyone who has *accepted* parenting knows this. I once asked a friend why she went to bed at 8:00 every night. Her response, *"I have a kid."* Now I understand—parents are exhausted from trying to maintain some semblance of order while doing the other 99 things that need to be done. A certain degree of order is necessary, but children need flexibility—they're taking in a lot of unfamiliar stimulation. They suffer from information overload.

They need to feel good about why they do things. This is how they internalize and develop their personality. As mentioned earlier in this chapter you need to treat children with respect and regard—the way you would want to be treated. To do this you may need to take some time to find new approaches—focusing on your children's strengths. A good example would be if a child was very boisterous.

"Suzie, that is a great outside voice, next time we go out I would like to see you use it. Since we are in the house right now, I would like to see if you know how to use your inside voice as well."

As you can see, you can take something that may seem negative yet turn it into something reasonably positive. You might even consider this a desirable trait. You can achieve your objective without hurting Suzie's feelings. It can take some time. And although a faster solution would be better, it's not something you were guaranteed as a part of the packaged deal (they also forgot to include the warning label: *at birth—hazardous to your sanity*).

2. Does your child enjoy being the center of attention or is he introverted and shy?

It's important to understand your child's disposition. For if a child is shy and uncomfortable with a lot of attention he may develop more slowly if he responds negatively to the attention. On the other hand, it may not always be wise to permit him to be withdrawn. The solution is to think in moderation. A child needs to develop social skills but if he is terrified by large groups, try not to make him the center of attention. Ease him into his social skills.

If a child likes the limelight, set it up as a reward. Tell him that the two of you could write a small play and perform it in front of a camera. Children love to see and hear themselves—whether it is looking at pictures, in the mirror or on the video. Be the potter and mold him to have a positive self image but let it be his self image. You have the power to influence your children—so go for it. Children need guidance and wisdom, this chapter highlights how a parent can achieve this process without completely stripping them of their sense of self. Give them a CHANCE to see the world through a clear and focused lens and watch them shine.

Homework

I Am The Potter, You Are My Clay

This assignment will help us learn how to prepare our children to understand the rules more clearly. First, we must assume they are not familiar with the rules unless the rules have been specifically laid out for them. Then we need to continue to repeat them to provide foundation.

For the best results, begin each morning by taking two minutes to explain the *new* rules that have been established. In order to stay on-track, write the expectations down prior to talking to your child. One important issue to note is that initially a child will not be comfortable with the change, you may need to give him/her extra time to accomplish the objectives. It would be best to start this new pattern on a weekend morning to give you the entire day to concentrate on behavior modification.

Examples:

> *"I want you to remember that we have to make our beds before we eat breakfast so if you will make your bed, I'll start breakfast."*

Note: Thank her for listening when she is done.

When it is time to leave the house to go shopping, tell your child in advance that he has five minutes before departure. If he is doing something like playing a game, this will give him enough time to wrap it up.

> *"Robert, we are going to grandma's in twenty minutes. We need to leave by noon so that we do not get stuck in traffic. If you are working on something or you need to get ready, this will give you enough time."*

Then in ten minutes repeat the fact that you must leave in ten minutes. This will allow the children the opportunity to finish up.

Journal Notes

CHAPTER TWO

KNOW, "NO, NO"

Know, "No, No"

Understanding why you say "no."

Children can interpret "no" as a parent saying, "I don't care about you," without actually hearing it. *"I don't have time...Maybe later...Not right now...You can't go...I can't right now...That's not right..."* These interpretations hold negative consequences for your children. When they hear "no" too often without *knowing* why, they'll internalize your response as one of not caring. If you are a parent who finds yourself in this predicament, then it's time to assess your motives.

The propensity to respond with "no," might just be a learned behavior (something your parents said to you). When children hear "no" too often and feel it's without *good* reason, they will eventually block out everything else you are saying and only hear "no." If you want them to understand what you are teaching them—only say "no" when it counts!

There are times, however, when "no" is absolutely necessary—boundaries and limitations must be established. Yet parents need to know why and how they say "no," then look for more positive alternatives. A good indicator which tells you whether your children are receiving your "no" positively or negatively is how they say "no" to you. If a child points her index finger in your face and says "no" loudly, she has heard "no" as punitive and is mirroring your attitude. If she hears, *"Honey—no, no, no,"* then she hears "no" in a more gentle and loving way. Do you ever yell "yes" when your child's done something right? Not usually—but maybe you should. Was your child's first or second word spoken, "no?" If so, guess what!

You may think that you are disciplining your children but when they constantly hear "no" they'll begin to internalize and lose their sense of self-worth. The following are some examples of how a child may interpret what she is hearing:

Parent's words: *"No, you can't watch that show, because I like to watch my soaps."*

Child's thoughts: *"My mom's needs are more important than mine, so I don't count."*

Parent's words: *"No, you can't have a bubble bath tonight."*

Child's thoughts: *"I am too much trouble and I am not worth it."*

Parent's words: *"No, I won't play with you, go play by yourself."*

Child's thoughts: *"I am not a lovable person or my dad would want to be with me."*

Are we mindlessly saying no because we truly do not value our children as individuals or is it that we are so caught up in everything that we *'think'* is important that we have forgotten where our priorities belong? My guess is that the latter holds true for most of us. We are so caught up in all of the *'responsibilities'* of adulthood that we have discarded the quality time we need with our children. We think, *"Well I can make time for them later, right now I have to get this report out."* Ask yourself, which of the two will be more important six months from now.

I remember a time when I was overwhelmed with the tasks of the day and I was in a really bad mood. My nephew asked if he could take a bath and I said, *"Yes but you can't have a bubble bath!"* His reply was, *"Why not?"* I sat there a moment—stumped. My response back was, *"There really isn't a good reason; so, I'll be right back with the bubbles."*

I was saying "no" without understanding why. Once I thought about it—I realized that I was letting my external environment (time constraints, responsibilities, etc.) control my behavior. I was concentrating on the negatives—no...don't...can't...When we focus our energy on all the "dos" and "don'ts" that we set for our children, we lose touch with the value and purpose of parenting. When the rules take precedence in a relationship, we lose sight of the most important goal—teaching our children to become healthy and happy human beings. We want to encourage them to grow and explore, so let's give them a CHANCE. We must not forget the intended purpose. The rules were originally designed to achieve the goals, right? We have lost the one thing that is most important—our focus.

Losing this focus reminds me of that song, *"Cats in the Cradle."* It's a story about a father who gets so caught up in his work and the fact that he needs to fulfill his employment responsibilities that he never makes time for his son. The boy always accepts the father's excuses and continues to idealize him. Throughout each verse the boy says, *"Someday, I'm gonna be like him, yea...You know I'm gonna be like him."* The father grows old and realizes he's all alone, so he tries to establish a relationship with his son. But what has happened is, the boy is too busy to be there for him. Result—the boy has learned his father's value system and doesn't have the time to be bothered. The end of the song says, *"As I hung up the phone, it occurred to me—my boy is just like me. He's grown up just like me."*

Don't let this happen to you. Nurture your children and make them understand that they are the *most* important part of your life above all else. This could be an investment that benefits your future as well as your children's.

"You're treating me like a child!"

Often children begin a transformation right before our very eyes yet we fail to recognize it fully. We see the physical transformations, but rarely do we perceive or acknowledge the emotional changes. Children need to explore their environment and cope with the struggles that complicate their lives. They may still be children but they are also emerging young adults.

As they grow they will want to have more control over their lives. When children are not given the CHANCE to grow with their bodies, they become teenagers with major attitudes (moreso than the average moody adolescent). If the conversations in your household are one-sided (and if *you* are that one side), then your children are not getting that opportunity. If you hear yourself using phrases starting with "I want...I said" and similar expressions, your children are probably hearing "no" without your actually saying it.

"I want...I need...I said..."

Who is getting left out here and is it fair? Adults sometimes forget that children are people too and that a relationship must be established with them. Relationship means consideration for all parties involved. The question is, do you consider what you have with your children a relationship or would you say it's more like a dictatorship? Stop and remember why you had children in the first place then ask yourself: "Is this why I wanted children?"

A friend once told me (after taking a psychology course) that she had completely failed as a parent. She felt she'd done everything wrong. We all feel this way at times, especially when we think about things we've said and done which we're not so proud of. However, belonging to the human race makes us prone to mistakes.

I want to stress two points here. (1) Taking a course is good but it doesn't mean the course has all the answers. We have to believe that we have made some contributions to our children and their lives. (2) Children are very forgiving and if we talk to them about our mistakes, there's a good CHANCE that they'll let us off the hook. If you feel that you are in the above category...you still have time...starting now!

Minimizing the word "no."

As mentioned earlier, there's always a place in a relationship for the word "no." Children need guidance and discipline. However, the law of opposites suggests that learning to minimize the negative will accentuate the positive—allowing more opportunities for children to grow.

You need to become more aware of what and how you say things to your children. It won't be easy, but no one said parenting would be. Rearranging how you say things, in order to create the positive will initially feel awkward. But simply limiting the child's options to those you can live with will be a good start. Children will try harder when they're driven in a positive manner. Good ways to promote positive behavior are to use phrases like:

(1) *"Always remember to put your dishes in the dish washer."*
(2) *"You need to walk through the house."*

Using the negative will encourage misbehavior:

(1) *"Don't forget to put the dishes in the dish washer."*
(2) *"Don't run through the house."*

The following are some examples to evaluate. Then use the desired methods on your children and watch the results.

Examples:

Which approach do you think is more effective?

(1) "What color is a frog, is it purple or is it green?"
(2) "A frog isn't purple. What color is a frog? No, a frog isn't blue. What color is a frog?"

The first response is always more effective. Giving children a choice will make them have a 50-50 CHANCE of getting it right. If they answer incorrectly, ask the question again, except this time say the word green louder and perhaps with an accepting smile. *"Is it purple or is it GREEN?"* If you have a younger child always say the correct answer, last because they will remember the last word more easily than the other words. The following conversation happened between my nephew and me (it reinforces the last word theory).

> One day Katlin and I were having a name-calling contest—just for fun:
>
> Me: "Katlin, you are a booger eating brat."
>
> Katlin: "I am not...a brat."

The objective is to build the child's self-confidence and help make positive accomplishments (not see how much they don't know). Give them choices versus using "no." No means wrong which equates to failure. If your boss kept telling you that you were doing your job wrong, you would probably internalize this as failure. It's not any different for children. We learn who we are as adults by the way we are taught as children.

Which of the following is the correct and most effective response?

(1) "Son, you don't eat your peas with a knife, you eat them with a spoon."

(2) "Son, do you eat your peas with a knife or a SPOON?"

Use some visualization. Show him a knife then a spoon. If you smile when you present the spoon, the child will probably pick the spoon because you have used some non-verbal communication. By giving your child a CHANCE to verbalize the correct answer, you have allowed him to independently make the right choice. The right choice equates to success. No matter how small it may seem to you, these are the things that build a child's sense of self-worth and self-regard.

Let Them State Their Case

A family is not, of course, a court of law. But sometimes it seems as if it ought to be seen as one. Our children see us as judge and jury, sitting high above them and making decision regarding their lives without necessarily taking into consideration what they might want. Before we say *no*, we should attempt to hear them out. My nephew often makes very valid points and I am forced to accept that I have made a mistake (which is very humbling). We can learn a fresh new approach to many of our problems if we just give our children the opportunity to state their case.

Giving our children a CHANCE to state their position will help them feel comfortable with making choices; not to mention building their sense of self-worth. It can be a big bad world out there and they need to learn how to cope before we release them to the wolves.

If we want to empower our children and encourage them at the same time to make the right choices—again, simply limit their options to those that we can live with. This way everybody wins—what a concept! These problems can range from the very simple to the most complicated.

Dad:	*"You can have one piece of gum."*
Child:	*"But I want two pieces."*
Dad:	*"I said you can have one."*
Child:	*"But I want two."*
Dad:	*"You can have one or none."*
Child:	*"I want one."*
Dad:	*"Good choice."*

This father allowed some debate yet set boundaries and limits that he and his child could both live with. The next example is a little more challenging because the mother must show the child that there is another point of view involved. Young children are by default egocentric (the world revolves around them). This is part of the development process. Often children have a difficult time understanding that others need consideration.

Child: *"I don't want to clean my room. Why does every decision in this house belong to you?"*

Mother: *"What do you mean?"*

Child: *"You always say, I want... I said... It's never what I want. I don't want to clean my room. You never listen to me, you're mean."*

Mother: In a gentle and caring way:

> *"When I drive you to baseball practice, is that something that I want? When I do the laundry, is that something that I like?"*

Child: *"No."*

Mother: *"I know that you need to go to ball practice so you never really have to say 'I want this' I just do it, right? It is important to me to have a clean house and it is important to you to go to ball practice so why don't we work together so that we can have both."*

This mother allowed her child to state her case but at the same time was able to show her that what she felt might have been somewhat unrealistic and untrue. Children often center the universe around themselves and are incapable of seeing situations from more than one perspective. This mother could have said, *"Just do what you are told."* But, is it more effective to show the child the reality? Help her internalize her choices and help her distinguish between right and wrong.

As the adult, you have liberties that children do not. It is your responsibility not to abuse that privilege. Think about what you say before you say it. Talk to your children the way you would like to be talked to. Know why and how you're saying "no"—it could mean a lot.

Homework

Know, "No, No"

This exercise will require that you begin minimizing the word "no" and "don't" from your vocabulary. The following is an example that can be used to change sentence structure.

Scenario:

A child is doing a chore around the house and makes a mistake. What will you say?

a. *"You are not supposed to put tile cleaner on the mirrors when you clean, it belongs in the tub."*

b. *"Did I remember to tell you that there is more than one cleaner to use in the bathroom? There are scrubbing bubbles for some things and window cleaner for others. You did such a great job using the scrubbing bubbles on the tub. The mirrors; though, should probably be cleaned with window cleaner."*

Starting now, listen to all the negatives that you may be saying and begin to rephrase sentences so that you are talking in the positive. It would be helpful to write down the negatives in order to see the frequency of the word "no." Remember to be encouraged by your past mistakes. It's your CHANCE to start over.

Journal Notes

CHAPTER THREE

"CATCH ME
IF YOU CAN!"

"Catch Me If You Can"

Catch your child being good.

Our children dare us to catch them being good. They desperately want attention and they are willing to do almost anything to get it. This includes, as many parents know, doing something negative just to be noticed. In a child's mind, *bad* attention is better than *no* attention. It seems obvious, then, that good attention is the more preferable, and we need to find ways to give it. The goal for this chapter will be to catch a child being *good*, in order to reinforce positive behavior.

It is important to understand that good or bad behavior is just that—*behavior*. Many parents tend to forget that it is not the *child* who is good or bad...it's his *behavior*. I hear many times:

> *(1) "Oh, Jimmy, you were such a good boy today."*
> *(2) "Sally, you were so bad at the store."*

The problem with these statements is that children will internalize that they are good or bad based on their behavior—when in essence it is the *behavior* that is good or bad and not them. If we do not want to destroy their self-esteem, we need to restate our sentences:

(1) "Oh, Jimmy, your behavior was so good today."
*(2) "Sally, you are a very good girl, but your behavior was
not so great today."*

This may seem like a lot of extra work but it is well worth the investment in order to build children's egos and give them the best self-esteem possible. We all can probably remember hearing our parents say something like:

*"I am the one in charge and I will not tolerate this type
of attitude."*

Conceptually, yes, they were the boss. But such an attitude did not serve to develop our sense of self-worth. Each generation of children has different needs from those of the proceeding. Today, children are concerned with gang violence, weapons in the school, AIDS and strangers. All of these pressures contribute to how they react to life.

We could continue using our parents' approaches, but the probability is that our children's generation will respond much differently than we did. If your child is like you then what worked for your parents may well work for your child, therefore use what works! If he is different, that approach will be ineffective. If the latter case describes your situation (i.e. your parents' methods are ineffective with regard to you own child), then you may only *think* that you are in charge. Consider this: Do you feel out of control, frustrated or annoyed when your relationship with your child is not on track?" Parents need to find a way to win the war while losing the battles. The key here is to determine how we really want to spend our time yet reach the desired results with the least amount of effort.

If you feel frustrated or annoyed by your child, you may see that your power and authority have been stripped from you by the little "apple of your eye." Then to make matters worse, you will realize that it was done without your knowledge or consent. You are the unsuspecting fly that has wandered into the spider's web. You have "unconsciously" given in to their control and have become entangled.

These precious little children have learned to "work you" and they fully understand what it takes to get their needs met. But, I would like to tell you that a child's behavior is not some calculating, manipulative ploy to destroy you (although it may seem as such). They have only learned through trial and error that a particular behavior *elicits* a particular response. Without guidance, a child will continue to look for creative ways to get what she needs. You can continue using these old ineffective parenting skills and get sucked into the chaos or you can seek other more positive alternatives.

First, remember who the "mature and rational" one is in this relationship (that's you). Then understand how much of your behavior impacts each situation and what a significant part it plays in the solution.

The behaviorist, Pavlov,[1] believed learning was accomplished through stimulus response. That is, associations could be made by cues in the environment. It can be argued that children have proven Pavlov's theory. A child who throws a temper tantrum has learned through experience that it takes approximately ten minutes to get the adult to give up. The child has achieved a two-edged victory. Though she has gotten your attention and gotten her way, she has also—unwittingly—succeeded in emotionally draining you. The resulting state of the parent—one of frustration and exhaustion—can lead to a very negative backlash against the child—leaving everyone thoroughly unhappy.

If you take the extra few minutes now to hear what your children are saying you might just like what you hear. Often they just need reassurance that you still care. Children have a great deal of determination. And furthermore, they possess a lot more energy and endurance than you do, which gives them an unfair advantage. Knowledge of this advantage hardens their will in seeking whatever is needed to meet their objective. You need to determine whether you feel their goals are sincere. Then you can decide whether you would like to attend to their needs immediately. If you attend now, you will save time and energy later.

---

[1] Pavlov was a behaviorist that tested stimulus response. He was able to show that dogs could associate a ringing bell with food. Each time the dog heard the bell ring, it began to salivate.

A little extra effort on our part now often saves time and frustration later.

I want to share some positive ways to redirect children's behavior that may prevent too many power struggles. Quite frankly, life will be much nicer when we learn to notice the *positive* things our children are doing rather than spending so much time concentrating on the *negative* things. It might seem like a lot of work, but I guarantee that some of the CHANCE techniques will help eliminate or at least minimize some of those undesirable behaviors.

"A child is more apt to want to make a good thing better rather than making a bad thing good."

Ways to make good things better:

1. *"I really like the fact that you made your bed without being told. Thank you."* (Giving a hug at this point would be icing on the cake.)

2. *"You know, I really appreciate it when you walk inside of the house. You are really trying hard."* (A child would enjoy an approving smile.)

3. *"You have been a great listener today. What do you say we go and get an ice cream?"*

4. *"It's okay that you didn't get all the answers right on the test. The important thing is that you tried hard*

and that is what really counts. I bet you'll do much better next time. You should be really proud of yourself."

There are so many ways to turn negatives into positives. An excellent approach is offered by the following example: Instead of saying, *"Don't forget what you need to do."* Try, *"Always remember what you need to do."* This emphasis on positive language is a subtle signal to children that *positive* is the way to go. Changing how you talk to your children will take an immense amount of practice. But once we get the hang of it, we'll love what we see. Attitudes are contagious!

Examples of negative reinforcement:

1. *"Why don't you listen for once?"*
2. *"Why do I always have to yell at you?"*
3. *"You never listen to a word I say."*

The subtle yet persistent effects of negative language will shape a child's self-image. Constantly using these negative expectations will program children for failure. Needless to say, there are even less subtle negative messages you need to guard yourself against. For example:

1. *"You are the laziest kid that I have ever met."*
2. *"I can't believe how stupid you can be."*
3. *"What are you—deaf? I swear you are unconscious."*

Children want to please their parents and they want to be recognized. Imagine that. Moreover, children will only live up to the expectations of their parents. If you tell them that they are lazy, then they will be lazy. If you tell them that they are great then they will be great. Believe it or not, you have more control than you realize. All you have to do is recognize it.

One effective way to correct your child is by using the *sandwich* effect. This is when you take "*constructive*" criticism and place it between two positive accomplishments.

> *"Courtney, I noticed that you got all the answers right on your math homework yesterday, I see so much improvement, you must be really proud of yourself. I spoke with your teacher today. She seems somewhat concerned that you might be having problems with your spelling. The fact that you are doing so well in math shows me that your heart is really into doing a great job, so maybe we can work together on your spelling."*

Doesn't that sound better than using the negative and saying:

> *"You got a "D" on your spelling test AGAIN. What is it gonna take for you to do better?"*

It's your choice. It can be said either way; however, I can almost guarantee that the latter approach is not likely to yield the best results for you or your child.

"It is easier to build a child than to repair an adult."

A good way to improve a child's positive behavior is to set aside at least fifteen minutes a day to dedicate to her without interruptions. This means that you must eliminate distraction—the telephone, television and anything else that could cause you to stray from your child. This nominal amount of time can generally be enough for a child. However, I would warn that if your child has been needy for attention, she may see this as an opportunity to take advantage of this *rare* occurrence and she may try and take more than the allotted time. If you can give more time, that's great! If you cannot, tell her that you will try later to fit in extra time.

When your time is limited, warn her in *advance* that you can only give her fifteen minutes. To be more successful, get a response. Be patient, you may have to repeat yourself.

"Danny, I can play with you for fifteen minutes, okay? Okay, Danny?"

Another positive way to give a child attention is to kiss and hug him without having any good reason—without a motive. Make it a goal to give him a minimum of five kisses or hugs a day. It is amazing how much that little investment will make in a child's behavior.

People have a great need for stimulation. Touch is both an

People have a great need for stimulation. Touch is both an emotional and physical need. Research has proven that the human body needs this stimulation. In one study infants were given all other basic needs (food, clean diapers and liquids—excluding touch), most developed a condition referred to as *"failure to thrive."* These babies literally lost their will to live. The findings suggest that the human body needs stimulation for it to *have* the will to survive.

I'm not trying to cause hysteria by suggesting that your children are on their death beds and you'd better act fast. What I am saying, though, is that if a lack of touch creates failure to thrive then a child who is loved through caress will be one who flourishes. Imagine the life enrichment you are nurturing—just by giving children those extra hugs and kisses. So give out those loveys—you will not be sorry.

Understanding why your child is misbehaving

Children often misbehave because they don't have the experience required to make choices. Parents need to draw upon their own knowledge to assist their children. This knowledge (learned from doing it the hard way) should provide your children with other alternatives. When you provide more positive methods for helping children make better choices, their behavior will change. As their behavior changes, you can acknowledge the positive (catch them dealing with a child's behavior.

One way to accomplish a proactive style to parenting is to repeat the rules prior to any negative behavior which you might anticipate. An example might be that your son always sneaks a cookie before dinner. You can easily nip this in the bud by reminding him *in advance* (proactive) that cookies are really good but dinner always comes first. When you wait until after he has eaten the cookie (reactive), your good intention has failed. If you need to go over those rules again and again and again—so be it. I cannot emphasize repetition enough. I cannot emphasize repetition enough. Repetition will reinforce expectation and promote better behavior.

Bad behavior can be in the eye of the beholder and may not really be bad behavior at all. A common phrase I often hear when talking to parents whose child is misbehaving is that: *"She knows better than that."* Children are not born with values. They develop and learn them through trial and error. What makes an adult think that a child could possibly know better? Most feel that children should know better because they know better. But the fact of the matter is, unless they are told *specifically* that it is not polite to stick their fingers in the peanut butter jar or up their friend's nose—they probably don't know that. The lesson here is *do not assume* that your child knows. The rule of thumb should be:

"If I didn't tell them the rules; there is a good possibility that they really don't know what the rules are."

Defining rules can help seize the moment and change many undesirable behaviors before they begin. An example: A child places a entire roll of toilet paper into the toilet—then flushes. You might view this behavior as deliberately vicious. Yet there may have been nothing calculating at all about it, still you viewed it as vicious and you lashed back in anger. You immediately freak out and scream at the top of our lungs. *"What—Tell me—What, were you thinking when you did this?!!!"* But the child may not have comprehended the consequences. Now the toilet begins to overflow (water and soggy paper covering the floor). The child is listening to this screaming as the water is swirling around his ankles. What do think is going through that child's mind?

Imagine you are at work and a piece of equipment that you are working on suddenly begins spewing oil because you hit the switch next to the power button. The boss immediately begins breathing down your neck and the harder you try to fix the problem—the larger the problem seems to get. The boss becomes irritated and all you can do is—panic. Children are not much different, they are just miniature adults—but they lack the experience to cope the way you do.

When you establish precedents, you need to clearly define for children everything—their rights, rules and responsibilities. This will ensure that they understand exactly what is expected from them. You must do this regularly because children are exposed to an overwhelming amount of information and it is difficult for them to absorb and *retain* everything.

Have you ever wondered why children like and need to hear the same story over and over again? Hence the importance of repetition. They need repetition to absorb everything. A child's language skills are developed by listening to the environment and generally this process takes more than one time of hearing it. We have all heard the saying, *"I learned it through osmosis."*

Children's thought process is much different than our own. Adults have command of the language process whereas children must depend of the limited knowledge they possess. We must be careful not to assume they understand everything. The following is a conversation I had with a small boy at the park.

Boy: "Is this your puppy?"

Me: "Yes. Do you have a puppy?"

Boy: "No. (Hesitates)
But I have a shovel."

Children will change their behavior as they change their goals.

If children are given the CHANCE to look toward the future with a positive outlook—their behavior will gradually transform. Hopefully this will meet their needs as well as your expectations— the best of both worlds.

Focusing on their goals will help you concentrate more on your children's positive attributes. As you help them accomplish their goals, they will develop a stronger and more positive ego. As a result, their outlook will improve, as they improve, so do you. It's a wonderful chain reaction that keeps going...and going...

A good way to prepare positive goal setting strategies for children is to begin each day as though it were your first. Giving yourself an opportunity to begin each day over will reduce your sense of being overwhelmed. This will brighten your outlook and help you find more positive behavior. Take each day and remember the strategies that worked and those that did not—then either apply them or throw them out.

A successful strategy may be when you have learned that your child likes polishing her nails. You can use this as a reward once she accomplishes her tasks. That reward is positive, so use it again. When you see that screaming at her isn't working, this is a strong indication that you need to find another way to handle her resistance. I like to refer to the old saying, *"Hey Doc, it hurts when I do that."*..."*Then don't that.*"This is the same concept. Quit using rewards and punishments that *do not* work.

Before you can think about changing behavior, you must first be able to recognize the problems at hand. Use the following steps to resolve conflict and you will have the battle half won. The combination of time, consistency and commitment make up the other half and no one can help with that—each parent is on his own.

Steps to conflict resolution

Step 1. Diagnose the problem—What is the difficulty?
Step 2. Generate a solution—Have a plan of action. You might need to try more than one.
Step 3. Evaluate the solution—Did it work?
Step 4. Make solution choices—If it worked, use it; if not, don't.
Step 5. Implement solution—Repeat this plan of action.

Many times a child's bad behavior is a direct result of a *symptom* created by a situation. The symptom is a *"transitory"* response (one of the moment). In simpler terms, he is experiencing some powerful feelings and is reacting with urgency. The behavior is only a result of his inability to react properly to the emotion and is not permanent. When a child is not taught to deal with his emotion, he will continue to repeat the same mistakes.

He is trying to cope with his anxiety and will need redirection through positive attention. He lacks the required knowledge, language and the experience to handle unknown situations. You may misunderstand the anxiety and identify it as defiance or disobedience but in reality it is just a case of the nerves. The energy is bouncing all over the place. You need to get to know your children before you write them off as brats. The answer can be very simple but if you are not looking in the right spot—you can misinterpret what your children are really trying to make you understand.

Time to get up!

If most of you are like me, getting your child ready in the morning is a horrendous and exhausting ordeal that takes an enormous amount of time and effort. We spend more energy concentrating on our time constraints (he still needs to brush his teeth, comb his hair, get dressed...) and forget to notice the good things (like he finished a shower, made his bed and fed the dog).

It is unrealistic to expect anyone to always stay positive and the truth is children drag their feet—especially in the morning. The reason for this procrastination is quite simple, in the minds of a child, waking up and getting ready equates to separation. She will be going to daycare or to school—the safety and comfort of *home* is disrupted. Everyone has places to go, things to do and deadlines to meet.

Knowing that she is going to be separated from her comfort zone reduces her motivation to move quickly. This especially holds true for younger children who are still emotionally dependent upon their parents. This disruption in turn produces a significant level of anxiety which causes procrastination to the fullest extent. Then the tension mounts. It's difficult for a child to perform under pressure. The dilemma is that you have to leave for work and your child has to be somewhat comfortable with that separation.

To combat this, find something that your child can look forward to such as going for a morning bike ride, reading her a favorite book or playing a special game. This way you can be positive with her and find good things to focus on. You want to find anything that makes that child want to soar into the day. For my nephew, getting dressed was something that he hated to do so I dressed him. For a long time, I fought it. I would think, "*He's old enough to dress himself, I'm too busy, why does he have to ruin my mornings.*" Then I realized that the separation anxiety that he was experiencing was causing these problems and not that he wanted to ruin my day. I began dressing him in the mornings and he woke up and he took better charge of the day.

He was old enough to dress himself but for some reason he found comfort in having me do it. I could have continued focusing on the negative and stayed frustrated but instead, I took five extra minutes and dressed him. This cut out the hassle thereby saving myself not only time but energy, while simultaneously creating a situation that is more positive. Parents in general need to concentrate more on a child's needs and forego the obsession to create an independent child. They will grow up fast enough. We need to give our children a CHANCE to develop a sense of safety and security at their own pace. In my particular case, if my nephew was sixteen and he still found a need to be dressed then perhaps a good therapist would have been needed but as it stands today (one year later) he dresses himself. It took time for him to want to dress himself but he did it. Remember, with every accomplishment there can be set backs—two steps forward, one step back. Although we progress slowly, we progress nonetheless and we are doing it with persistence and love. This combination will prevail.

We all get tired and sometimes we lose our patience; but, it's our responsibility to at least try to understand what our children need. We have to concentrate less on how they perform and more on what is going to make them become more confident and self-assured individuals. We will not always see the effects now, but we will definitely see the results later.

Do you know what your child is really trying to say to you?

One day at the park, I observed a small boy trying to swing. He called out to his mother:

Boy: *"Could you push me mommy?"*

Mother: *You know how to swing yourself, you don't need me to do it."*

Boy: *"Please mommy, just once."*

The mother hesitated for a moment and appeared agitated but came over to swing him anyway. The boy said, *"Thank you mommy."* In this scenario the mother was right in recognizing her son's ability to swing himself but that was not the issue. The boy needed reassurance and was saying, *"Mommy, I need you to remind me that you love me."* And initially, the mother was saying, *"I don't want to right now."* When the boy was saying thank you, he was really saying, *"I love you for loving me. I really needed that."* You can give the few extra positive minutes in advance and create a more pleasant environment that will set a more positive stage for your children.

The best gift

Most parents feel that it is important to provide a lot of material goods to their children. Unfortunately, this places parents in a position where they are constantly giving to their children and receiving little to nothing in return (i.e. respect, cooperation, or appreciation). If you are one of these parents, you may want to rethink your priorities, that is, if you care to get any type of return on your investment.

The simplest way to create an environment which is more conducive to changing behavior is to replace material items with quality time. Positive time affords you the opportunity to discover who your children are (and you might even enjoy what you learn). Believe it or not you are the best gift that you can give to them. Children may not initially feel comfortable with this new change. They have grown accustomed to filling their emotional needs through video games, the best new clothes, and expensive new fads—things that can never really satiate those needs.

You'll need to ask yourself whether or not you want your children to identify their self-image through material items or through you. If you choose the latter, trust yourself and use consistency and longevity to win them over. Think about it—would you have them remember the $200 jacket you bought them or the time you took them camping and you built the most awesome campfire together?

One way to increase time with children is to limit the amount of hours they are permitted to watch television. You will be amazed at how much more they will talk to you once they get into the routine. But again...I would warn that changing your behavior will seem foreign and perhaps uncomfortable initially—for everyone. They may be thinking in Sci-Fi (the invasion of the body snatchers), *"Who is this person inside my father's body and what did he do with my dad?"*

You also need to begin catching your children doing good things. This can be accomplished by showing an interest in your child's school work. Ask her to actually show you what she has accomplished versus asking her whether the homework is completed. If you express an interest in her accomplishments, there is a good CHANCE that she will also begin showing an interest. When you are viewing the homework, you may also learn about a lot of your child's strengths. The next natural progression would be to compliment the work (i.e., her ideas are great, the penmanship is neat, or her creativity is like yours).

We have to mold and build children's egos and what better way than to enhance their love of self—which in turn will promote their sense of worth. Your children need you to care about what they do. So start trying to catch them in the act!

Another gift you can give your children is to share some of the inadequacy that you felt as child. Children perceive adults as all-powerful and all-knowing; therefore, they are reluctant to share their inadequacies. The best way to understand children is to let them understand you. They will not only get a kick out of hearing your stories but...they will relate to you much better too. It will definitely be a humbling experience, but what the heck! I would caution you to not use the stories like, *"I walked three miles to school uphill both ways in the winter without shoes."* Just use the ones that made you vulnerable. The goal is for them to relate to you. You want them understand how you felt as a child and not to show them that you had it tougher.

Humans learn about life through watching the people around them. Just like a lion cub who learns to hunt by going along for the kill, a child learns from watching and experiencing the life around him. Observing others is how we get our ideals, our values, our strengths, and our *weaknesses.* Parents must break the facade that they are perfect. This only sets up unrealistic expectations and goals for their children. If a child compares himself to this facade, he will develop a sense of inadequacy because of these *imperfections.* Showing vulnerability is not necessarily all bad. You need to let them know who you are and that you are not flawless.

Homework

"Catch Me If You Can!"

Changing criticism into praise is the purpose of this exercise. On average, it takes approximately three months to change a behavior (depending upon the severity of the change). This might seem like a long time; but, I promise if you donate three months now, your investment will pay off. Write down everything that you say to your children when you talk to them, especially if it is a reaction to their behavior.

Wait until the children are in bed and you have had time to relax, then review what you said to them. Then take the criticisms and ask yourself, "Would I want anyone to speak to me this way? How could I change these criticisms into praise." Next look at your praises and give yourself praise for taking that extra moment to be positive. The goal here will be to compare your worksheets on a weekly basis for one month. Each week reducing the criticisms and increasing the praise. This will take a concerted effort; but, once you are aware of your comments this will be much easier. Refer back to the chapter for examples if you need them. Good Luck!

Journal Notes

CHAPTER FOUR

"HEY, I'M TALKING TO YOU!"

"Hey, I'm Talking To You!"

Learning How To Speak To Your Children

Communicating with children isn't always easy. You know exactly what you want to say to them; unfortunately, you aren't always successful in conveying it—even when you think you are.

The problem with communication is not so much how one relays the message as it is how the recipient *interprets* it. We can possess what we think are the greatest communication skills in the world, yet find that the message we were sure we conveyed still got mixed up. The reason this happens is that the recipient's emotions, values and beliefs become involved in how he interprets the message.

Emotions, values, and beliefs act as filters, each of which plays a role in the child's interpretation. Thus, the message gets muddled and is not received so clearly as it was intended.

Let's say, for example, that your child gets into a fight at school and gets beaten up. Returning home, he feels humiliated and vulnerable. You (innocently) ask him to take out the trash. Without warning, he becomes unglued and says something like:

"You always treat me like I'm some kind of slave! Why do I have to do everything?"

It's natural that a parent's first reaction is filled with anger because *this* kid has just attacked you. A knee-jerk reaction may be to lash back.

"Who does this kid think he is—taking THAT attitude with me?"

What happens now, unfortunately, is that this child is placed right back in the position of losing. Not only has he been beaten up at school... now he has had the humiliation reinforced at home. This type of negative reinforcement will teach him that he is not worthy of being treated fairly and that he cannot control his own environment.

He perceives you as a controlling power monger (always talking down to him) but all you wanted was to have the trash taken out. This is not an unreasonable request—just bad timing.

The best approach to prevent issues of a similar nature from recurring is to learn to read your child's body language. For what a child is *not saying* is much more important than what he *is* saying.

Understanding your child's body language is not so difficult as it might seem. What a child is feeling can easily be read through gestures, facial expressions, body movement, physical posture and eye contact—all of these say important things about what's going on inside her head. All you have to do is tune in and watch. Don't always believe what you hear, because a child may say one thing, yet with her body may express the complete opposite.

When you see that your child has her head down appearing quiet and is using very little eye contact, there is a strong possibility that she is experiencing sadness or disappointment. If you ask her, "What's wrong?" She will probably respond with—"*Nothing.*" (Predictably, this will be said without making any eye contact and with a low monotone voice). At this point, a parent may drop the subject simply because he is listening to the verbal communication and not seeing that there truly is a problem.

Unfortunately, the problem has now been further exacerbated. The child feels alone and misunderstood by her parents. Why? Because the parent did not recognize the *real* problem.

Children believe that their parents are all-powerful and all-knowing. They want their parents to see the problem without being told. After all—parents are always right, aren't they? A child who has gotten beaten up at school needs his parent to see what's going on.

In order to see into your child's feelings, use an application which I refer to as the RAVE technique. It means, *Recognize, Acknowledge,* and *Validate* his feelings, then *Elicit* a response from him. Often you can see when your child is hurting or experiencing other emotions but recognizing this isn't enough, you must follow through with the other three steps to complete the communication cycle to successfully reach resolution.

Once you see that your child is having a problem, *acknowledge* it by saying something like, "*I can see that you angry.*" This takes the responsibility for acknowledging the feelings away from the child. Next, *validate* him by saying, *"I understand how you feel, when I'm angry, I sometimes really want to lash out at others too."* This puts you in a position that says I am like you and I appreciate how you feel. Lastly, you must *elicit* a response and communicate. This is critical. Communication requires two—get down on his level, talk *with* him, not *to* him, then help him look for other alternatives to the inappropriate reactions. The last thing you want to say to him at this point is, *"Take out the trash."*

When you take the time to RAVE about your children, obtaining your objectives—like garbage removal—will only be a matter of timing. Here is an example of a more effective way of communicating:

> *"Gee, I can tell by the look on your face that you must have had a very hard day. I bet you could use a break."*

Then gently give him a hug. Later—ask him how he feels. Once the mood shifts in a more positive direction, make the request. If the mood does not shift, tell him you understand that he had a rough day so *you* will take the trash out *this time.* You will earn the child's gratitude—for a few minutes anyway. But you will be amazed at how much difference even a few minutes will make.

I remember an incident at work where I was having a terrible afternoon and a co-worker forgot to do what she was supposed to. Consequently, I had to do it. I was agitated because my day was messed up and now I had to do something that I didn't feel I had time for. When she returned, I snapped at her, then I walked away. Rather than fighting with me, this lady went to the liquor store and bought two small Long Island Iced Teas and brought them to my office. I asked her why she was doing this and she said, *"You usually don't get angry like that, so I thought maybe you might need a break."* I have never forgotten that. She had every right in the world to snap back at me, but instead she *recognized,* and *acknowledged,* my feelings. Her act of kindness made me feel *validated*—she cared enough to overlook my attitude and allowed me to vent my frustrations without retaliation. Guess what...my anger subsided (she *elicited* a response). The anger was replaced with gratitude and appreciation.

Let's go back to the trash scenario for a moment and use it to demonstrate how a child can misunderstand what the parent is saying. If the child is feeling sadness and humiliation and is preoccupied with the events of the day, then a comment about the trash will more than likely send him over the edge. He immediately puts up his defense wall and storms off.

You thought that you had only asked him to take out the garbage but he had interpreted it as a criticism and not as a request. Then you get upset and say, *"Hey, I'm talking to you."* When you speak to your children in this tone you usually do not get the desired results—not without a hassle anyway.

Your child probably wasn't ignoring you, intentionally. If you weren't *recognizing, acknowledging* and *validating* his emotions, it's possible that you misinterpreted his *(elicited)* reaction as defiance. Thus begins a cycle of misinterpretations and misunderstandings that end in everyone getting frustrated and angry.

As a parent, though, it is your responsibility to ensure that communication is *working*. You are the adult and the one with the experience and the knowledge. You do not and will not have all the answers, but you have to at least try to find as many alternatives as possible. The next few sections will illustrate some techniques to help you read your child.

When your child is lying

Eye contact is difficult for anyone who is attempting to lie and is particularly difficult for a child because of her lack of experience and her natural innocence. A child will shift her eyes from side to side or perhaps even rub them. She will stare at her hands and shuffle her feet to avoid making eye contact. Once you are tuned in, most lying is obvious.

There are many ways to react to a child who is lying. But there are two clear options a parent can choose. First, confront her right away and tell her that you know that she is lying and that you do not appreciate it. Second, you could say something to this effect:

"You know, you have always been really honest with me and you have always told the truth. Something in what you said doesn't feel quite right, so I would like you to try and tell me over again, perhaps I misunderstood what you just said. Because I know that you would not be dishonest on purpose."

The second option throws all the burden of the truth onto the child. That is, option one gives her an opportunity to get defensive and fight you. But option two tells her how much you want to trust her, and implies the gravity of her lie to you. The chances are strong that she will not want to repeat the lie. Option two also gives her a way to wiggle out of something she might regret. When a child uses option two, use it to your advantage and follow through with praise:

"Thank you, now I feel much better that I understand you correctly."

In the case where the child repeats the lie—say:

"Gee, I think that maybe you are a little confused and so maybe you need to think about what you just said because I know deep in my heart that you would not lie to me on purpose."

Children do not want to disappoint their parents and will do almost anything to please them. If your child is still lying, this can be considered blatant disrespect and you will have to resort to a more direct approach. However, use it as a last resort because when a child can correct a situation herself, she can internalize and accept the situation more easily and the effects will last longer.

When your child lies excessively, you might ask yourself what his motivation is. Perhaps the consequences of telling the truth are too scary to him. Some parents will impulsively blow up when a child has done something wrong and he fears their reaction. It becomes *safer* to lie than to be honest. Children respond more favorably when they can count on their environment. Younger children are notorious for telling on themselves, but as they grow, they may fear that the consequences of telling the truth are too great. For example:

Dad: *"Did you hit Sarah?"*

Sammy: *"Yes."*

Dad: *"YOU KNOW HOW I FEEL ABOUT YOU HITTING YOUR SISTER!!! WHY DO YOU DO THINGS YOU'RE NOT SUPPOSED TO DO?"*

If you *really* want the truth, then reward it. If you want justice I'd still recommend rewarding the truth. Children need to know that it is NOT okay to hit their siblings, yet feel safe enough to tell their parents the truth. It is important to administer punishment in order for children to understand that there are consequences to everything they do. Yet the consequence should be less severe when the child tells the truth. I consider the following alternative solution more appropriate to the above situation. Maybe this way everyone can win.

Dad: *"Did you hit Sarah?"*

Sammy: *"Yes."*

Dad: *"Thanks for being honest."* (Now Dad turns to Sarah, kneels down and kisses her then ask her if she's okay. He lavishes her with attention—ignores Sammy—but not in a punitive way).

Recall that when a child does something he knows is wrong, it is often just a ploy to get the parent's attention. Sammy, in this scenario, will see who gets the attention. And the parent will meet his objective! You have reinforced telling the truth yet at the same time not rewarded the behavior. It's a good bet that next time—Sammy will try to get the attention another way, because he has seen that Dad is not going to react. Later, Dad can reinforce Sammy by rewarding him for telling the truth. For example: When his wife gets home from work, he could greet her at the door (making sure Sammy is within ear shot) and say something like, *"Sammy, told the truth today, even when he knew he might get in trouble. ISN'T THAT GREAT? I was so proud of him."*

Sammy will feel so good about himself and take that piece of praise and file it in the back of his mind. What do you think he will do next time to get your attention?

When your child doesn't want to listen

It is easy to recognize your child's body language when she is ignoring you. Say for example, you are telling your child something that she does not want to hear or something she obviously does not agree with. Her physical reflex will be to scratch behind her neck close to the ear or lightly play with her ears. What you have just witnessed is body language at its finest and the funny thing is the child is totally unaware of what she has just told you. Although this is unconscious to the child—mentally, it is her body's quiet way of saying, *"I can't hear you, nana nana na na."*

Another nonverbal move is when a child crosses his arms and looks away. He says in this way, *"I am closed and the words you are saying can't get in."* Kids will roll their eyes to show that they are not listening or that they disapprove of what you are saying. Your impulse may be to lose your temper but that isn't good for anyone. So if you are ticked off—give yourself a time-out, come back and work it out once you are calm.

One communication problem I must continually combat is repeating myself over and over and over again. One day, I got really mad and screamed at my nephew. His response was, *"You don't have to talk to me like that."* And I yelled, *"YES I DO, BECAUSE WHEN I SAY IT NICELY... YOU...DON'T...LISTEN!!"* No matter how many times I tried screaming, it didn't work. Each time, I only felt more frustrated.

Then I asked myself: *"Self, what can you do to get better results?"*

What I decided was to tell him:

"You know, I get really frustrated when I have to continually repeat myself, so for the next two hours every time you say something to me I will not respond until you say it three times. If you want a glass of milk, you will have to ask me three times. If you want to go to the park, I am going to ignore you until you say it at least three times. And when you want to show me something, you will have to ask me over and over again. I want you to see how frustrating it is."

He didn't like it, but he got the point. There are still times when he doesn't listen—that goes with growth and asserting independence—but it happens with less frequency. Think about it, as you grew, didn't you want to be independent from your parents? Try to remember and appreciate how difficult it is to be a child. You've been there and done that...now reflect and remember.

It's important to stay calm and help your child understand how it feels to be the adult. You can accomplish two things: (1) you can *recognize, acknowledge* and *validate* your own feeling and (2) you can teach your child a lesson in empathy—a quality trait which many people have lost. To be effective, it is important that you always discuss the child's feelings with him after the consequences. Immediate feedback will promote better communication and heal hurt feelings. If he verbalizes his issues, he is more likely to internalize them more easily.

When your child is sad

Children do not want to admit that they are sad...especially when it's because their feelings were hurt. This is something that you will have to pry out of them. As the parent, it is your job to recognize your child's needs. Sad children keep their hands intertwined and locked together and they'll look down toward the ground, avoiding any eye contact. If you look carefully, these motions are screaming out at you—you just need to take the time to read them. The worst thing that you can do to block communication is ask your children a closed-ended question, that is, a question that only gives them the option of answering either "yes" or "no." Two examples of closed-ended questions are:

(1) "Do you feel okay?".
(2) "Did you have a nice day?"

Their inadequate language skills often make children resistant to communication. Consequently, children will generally respond to these type of questions with a yes simply because it is easier than trying to explain no. The problem here is they really do mean no. A more appropriate response is,

"Gee, you look really sad today. Whatever is bothering you must be really important for you to look so sad. I know that when I'm sad, I like to talk about it so I can feel better."

By phrasing the sentence in this manner, what you have said is: *"I know something is bothering you and talking about it can help you feel better"*. This takes the responsibility of telling you that he feels bad away from him and helps open communication lines. Remember to RAVE. You are *recognizing, acknowledging* and *validating* his feelings.

If he doesn't want to discuss his feelings right away, don't give up! Give him some time then ask him again later. But always, always *elicit* a response. Whatever caused the sadness—did not simply go away just because the subject was dropped. Life is very hectic and time seems limited, but if you take that few extra minutes and read his body language...you will help him build his sense of self-worth.

Your non-verbal messages

Equally important in the quest to understand and communicate with your children is how your non-verbal messages speak out to them. *Your* tone, attitude and body language communicate as much to them as theirs do to you. Children will draw their own conclusions when there isn't enough information provided to clear up the situation. Some parents may think that children don't understand what is going around them...but they really do.

When you are busy and you focus on everything else that *seems* important (except for your kids), you are sending out a terrible message to them. The signals are telling them that they are at the bottom of the priority list. When you get caught up in all the nuts and bolts in life and forget to listen, you may find yourself mechanically responding to your children (and they know you are not listening). Don't be surprised to experience something like...

Child: *"Can I borrow your shaving cream for an experiment?"*
Parent: *"Oh sure, honey, just be neat."*

Child takes newspaper and neatly places it on the floor then she proceeds to shave the cat.

Parent: *"What are you doing?"*
Child: *"You told me to be neat."*

If you really want to be true to your children, take time and truly listen for them. By not expressing an interest in them (whether intentional or not), you are in essence saying,

"What you do is not important to me therefore you are not important to me."

It is difficult to dedicate your every waking moment to your kids, but prioritizing will help. Remembering who and what is important will help you learn about your children and who they really are. The results are quite rewarding.

Gender Identification

We learn to identify and communicate through observation of a same-sex person. One of my personal examples, regarding the dynamics of gender identification, was the time I wanted my nephew to learn to cook and love it! He went through the motions, but he lacked enthusiasm. Then one afternoon a male friend of mine took care of him. Together, they prepared dinner. For the next week, my nephew couldn't wait to get into the kitchen. My nephew watched my friend and learned through observation that as a guy it can be fun to cook.

Gender identification is one of the most powerful interactive forms of communication that our children learn from. Unfortunately, more than half of the families in the United States today are headed by single parents—cutting out a significant portion of the parent/child interaction that goes into building the child's identity. I am part of this phenomenon and although I do the best that I can...I am only one person. This situation can be difficult for any parent, but it is particularly difficult for a parent who must raise a child of the opposite sex.

Half of the role-modeling structure and genetic makeup for children is missing. As hard as you may try—one parent cannot satisfy all their emotional needs. With the breakup of the family, children have lost a portion of "who they are." Children learn to interact and communicate by watching others. If the same-sex parent is missing from the picture—it will be much more difficult for the gender identification process to occur.

This book is primarily geared toward the "average" family (whatever that means) but to make an over-exaggerated point, I want to share my experience as domestic violence counselor. The dynamics of domestic violence show the extremes of everything, but especially how important our behavior is regarding gender identification when raising children.

Studies show that when a young boy witnesses his father beat his mother, he is 700 times more likely to grow up and find a partner to beat. A young girl who witnesses the same abuse will in all probability grow up and seek out a batterer. Not because he or she wants to but because that is what they have learned is *normal.*

What does that tell us about the importance of gender identification? We must understand that everything our children experience becomes a part of who they are. It's our responsibility to ensure that we can provide (to the best of our ability) the healthiest and safest environment possible for our children.

The rise of single-parent households and the increase in youth violence suggest that the absence of positive gender role modeling has had a profound effect on our young children. Most of these families are being run by single mothers and although our daughters are affected greatly by the loss of a father, they have their mothers to identify with. But, our sons have lost a part of who they are.

Fortunately, there are resources in the community that are

sensitive to these needs and can provide families with some help. One organization is the Big Brother/Sister program. My nephew has a Big Brother who has made a significant difference in his and my life. This program provides an opportunity for Katlin to interact and communicate with the same sex and gives me time to myself. Other programs available are Parents without Partners, YMCA & YWCA, churches and MOPS (Mothers Of Preschoolers). Check your community for other valuable resources. You will be surprised at what is out there—and also surprised at the positive contribution such resources can make.

One thing I want to stress is, no matter how great a parent may be, children need to be exposed to other people with whom they can identify. Let's do what we can to make sure that those they identify with are positive!

Concrete Thinkers

Younger children are concrete thinkers, everything is taken literally. Their minds have not become accustomed to the abstract. Consequently, their thought process is not very flexible. Two examples come to mind for me:

(1)   Me: *"If you would like to spend the whole day in your room just make me mad ONE more time."*

My nephew: *"Why would I want to spend the day in my room?"*

(2)   My nephew: (While viewing a Disney World commercial at the age of three), *"Can we go there?"*

Me: *"Maybe when you are five."*

On Katlin's fifth birthday, he announced to the family that we were leaving that day for Disney World. I said, *"Where did you get that idea?"* He said, *"You told me we could go when I was five. And now I'm five."* He would not let the issue die, and—three months to the day—we left for a sunny vacation in Florida and spent the day with Mickey and Goofy. The lesson I learned was never be flippant with children—they will take it literally. Trust me on this one, or it could cost you big bucks.

"I" vs. "You"

A very basic way to improve communication skills with children is to change sentence structure. You can do this by replacing the word "you" with "I". Using "you" statements will generally put anyone on the defensive and will create barriers to communication. In order to restructure sentences though, you will need to take some time to think about what you *really* want to say before you say it. Restructuring may be a little difficult initially, but once you get the hang of it, it will be easier. Like other behavioral changes, it is something that must be practiced. The following are some examples of how to change sentence structure.

Rephrase this sentence:

"YOU really make me angry when YOU leave YOUR clothes all over the floor."

To something like:

"I really feel uncomfortable when I see clothes on the floor. What can we do about this?"

Rephrase this sentence:

"YOU are always dragging your feet when it's time to go ."

To something like:

" I know that I'm picky about leaving on time, and that sometimes it seems like I am being over-sensitive, but I feel that I have shared that punctuality is important to me."

As you can see from the last example, changing sentence structure can exhaust more time and energy. But, using 'I' statements will help drop a child's defenses. I can almost guarantee, without a doubt, that using 'You' statements in such situations will only cause a child to tune *you* out.

No one likes to be personally attacked and although you are trying to make a point, the person receiving the information will not turn her little receiver on. She will be closed to any suggestions you may have if she does not feel a certain degree of mutual respect.

As mentioned earlier in this chapter, the person sending the message may think she is doing a great job, but if the receiver interprets the message differently...the probability is that your true intent may not have come through. If you want your children to be comfortable listening to you, then talk to them in a manner which is conducive to picking up the *right* message with good reception. Use the techniques in this chapter to help you understand how your children talk to you and how you talk to them. There's so much to be said and so much to be listened to if you just look hard enough.

Homework

"Hey, I'm Talking To You."

This next assignment will require you to ask your child open-ended questions versus closed-ended questions. This exercise will take 10 minutes every night. For best results, establish a particular time every evening, since this will help develop consistency and build routine. If a child anticipates an event it will be much easier for you. The time could be set for after dinner or homework or at a prescribed time like 6:00 p.m. Whatever you choose, just ensure consistency. Children need routine.

Example of open-ended question would be:

"Tell me something that happened today that was really exciting."

Example of closed ended question would be:

"What did you do today?" The child is likely to respond, "Nothing"

You can ask questions regarding issues such as:

1. Are there any activities in school this week that are good to discuss or what happened at school today?
2. What type of homework do they have?
3. What their teacher taught them today? Who is their favorite teacher and why?
4. Who is their best friend and why is that person so special?
5. What is the one thing your child likes to do with his/her mom or dad?
6. What did they have for lunch today?" (Perhaps you can relate some school lunch stories with them.)

Journal Notes

CHAPTER FIVE

ANGER:

RIGHT

OR

RESPONSIBILITY?

Anger:
Right or Responsibility?

"Is Anger Wrong?"

This chapter highlights the pros and cons regarding anger and ways of coping with both children's and parent's anger. I will share anecdotes which show some differences in the way anger can be handled to make it more effective. Then I will share how these different approaches affect children. There are some things that ought never to be said in anger, equally important is the strength it takes to overcome the aftermath of those hateful words. This chapter will also show the importance of taking responsibility for anger and ways of resolving a situation when you realize your anger was unjust.

But, as I said, we are not the only ones who get angry. I will discuss children's anger, and show how to give them acceptable ways to express their feelings. Then I will suggest methods to minimize inappropriate anger—helping both the parent and child cope more effectively with the situation at hand.

Be Careful—Somebody's Watching!

I saw a very well dressed woman one day at the entrance of a large toy store. She and her four children were entering the store. What struck me was that she was walking backwards bent over staring and growling at her daughter. She looked like some lunatic trying to rationalize with a wall.

Prior to becoming a parent, I would have looked at this person and instantly drawn the conclusion that she was a terrible and hurtful parent. Knowing what I know now, my reaction was different. I sensed that she had experienced an entire day of craziness and her patience was *maxed* out. Think about it: do you ever find yourself bent over walking backwards and snarling rabidly like a raving maniac when you are walking and talking with an adult? Probably not. It is amazing how being with a two-year-old can transform an otherwise stable and rational person into someone who looks like she has never formulated a complete sentence in her entire life.

This woman was not abusive—only frustrated. But the threshold between frustration and abusiveness can sometimes be a very fine line. It is essential that we understand where that threshold lies for us, and that we recognize the need to call a time-out before we get to the point of "losing it."

If you find yourself babbling like a complete idiot, look around, someone could be watching—you might find your actions/reactions written in a book someday.

Bad Anger Vs. Good Anger

Anger is a natural emotion, just as sadness and happiness are. Children learn brilliantly what buttons to push, and they are constantly challenging us. It is the parent's responsibility to be consistent and loving. Sometimes that will mean getting angry. Our children need and desire boundaries—even when those limitations may not be to their immediate advantage. Yet we must be careful not to abuse our responsibility as parents by getting angry with our children unjustly. We really need to be conscientious about setting parameters for them. Kids are not born with boundaries...they must learn them from us. It is our responsibility to make them the *right* boundaries.

I met a man at the park whose little girl was petting my dog. He approached me and grunted, *"Aren't kids the biggest pain in the butt?"* His anger and hostility took me aback. I responded with something like, *"Oh, I think kids are great. Your daughter has been quite the young lady, so sweet and polite."* His response, *"That's cuz I beat her."* I was horrified and utterly speechless by his response.

Does being a parent give us a license to berate or yell at our children anytime we please? Of course not! This man's disposition was damaging and harmful to his daughter. It is our responsibility to be firm yet fair; consistent yet yielding. We must practice good judgment.

You are now entering...the time zone.

Think really hard about something that made you feel insecure as a child. You may have felt ugly, stupid, lazy or uncoordinated, for instance. Now, consider why you felt that way. I would bet that someone had told you one or all of these things. That message was registered and filed away into your self-consciousness.

Often, such negative messages are played with persistent regularity. I would ask you—once again—to think how those messages affect you today. These negative messages were recorded into your tiny little head. The imprinted messages are like worn out recordings to really bad songs which were played over and over again.

Although you have become an adult, you don't lose the messages that have been created. You will often continue feeling badly about issues that have affected you as a child simply because someone told you so.

If you still maintain some of those feelings, the ball is in your court...you can continue to accept those messages and pass the same messages onto your children or you can change them! Now is the time to recognize and appreciate everything that you say to them.

Anger may need to be applied for the purpose of teaching children boundaries. It is the adult's right to establish these limitations but it is also their *responsibility* to ensure that the anger is for the right reasons. Parents have the potential to either build or destroy their egos—that's a lot of power to hold—use it with caution.

Again, you were not born with your self-image—you simply learned through past experiences (it's a progression). The great news is that the power to change the behavior is there. You have a CHANCE to erase the old negative messages and replace it with a new and more positive recording. You can be your own recording star and if the recording is a hit perhaps you could cut your own album, tape or CD.

Bad Anger Leads to Negative Outcomes

The following are words that should never be said when you are angry with your children:

1. *"You stupid dummy."*

Never, never name call in anger. You will destroy the entire core of your children by using this practice. This serves only as a self-gratifying weapon and does not achieve anything. Your frustration is only temporary but the damage inflicted can be permanent. Furthermore, you are yourself probably breaking the very rule that you've established for your kids by name calling.

Recently at a musical, I heard a grandmother yelling at her

granddaughter. She was annoyed because her granddaughter said that she could not see the people on stage. Her grandmother proceeded to physically shove her down into a seat in the front row THEN in a loud voice said, *"What a pain in the ass."* I wanted to run over and wrap my arms around that little girl and tell her that she was the most precious thing that I had ever seen and to tell her that her grandmother was nothing but a mean, old battleax. Imagine what that child must of thought about herself. After all, isn't the adult always right? Isn't that what we teach children?

"Respect your elders...Do as you are told...Don't talk back..."

What will this child believe of herself? It is only the exceptional child who can see an adult for who she really is—most children will assume that the adult is right. And that assumption leads to the internalization that they are *bad.*

Each child's emotional growth is like a set of bricks—each new experience creates a foundation for the next. If children are continually criticized, that foundation will become brittle; and eventually, it will collapse. If the bricks are not reinforced with a stronger material (patience and encouragement)—the wall will come tumbling down.

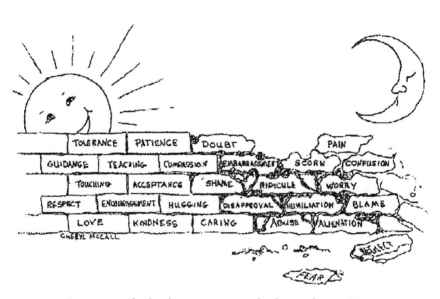

2. *"It's your fault that I am in a bad mood"* or *"You have ruined my entire day."*

Children have no control over how *we* handle *our* emotions. If our day is ruined, it is because we choose to only look at the negative side of things. If we find ourselves raving or livid about some juice our child has spilled on the carpet, it might be instructive to attempt to put things in perspective. Where I live, there is a residence for disabled individuals nearby. One day when someone or something *ruined* my day, I took a drive to calm myself. I saw across the street a severely handicapped person in a motorized wheelchair attempting to cross the street at the light. Suddenly my own problems paled...Here was someone with real obstacles and difficulties, who had the courage and tenacity to go out into the world. Next time we find ourselves ticked off because our child has spilled some juice on the carpet—go out and watch the world. Most of us are blessed with good health. There isn't anything in my opinion more sobering than witnessing these extraordinary people. Can you imagine how their day must feel? I bet they wouldn't base a "bad day" on something so insignificant as a spilt glass of juice. If an incident like this will not matter in six months—it doesn't matter now. We really ought to follow that proverbial advice to lighten up, loosen up and smell the flowers. Life is too precious to waste by blaming the world for our bad moods.

The world is made up of two kinds of people when it comes to controlling circumstance in life. Those who believe their environment controls their lives and those who believe they control their environment. The former possess an 'external locus of control.' They blame everything and everybody but themselves for their problems and shortfalls. They believe they have no control over their own destiny. As parents, such a person might say to himself, *"It's not my fault that I am a bad parent—my father criticized me."* This person's judgment is limited and his options are fewer because he cannot look beyond what the environment provides him. Basically, there isn't any accountability.

Those who take control of their own lives and try not to blame anyone for their problems—they are on the other side of the fence, with an 'internal locus of control.' *"What I do to my child is my responsibility—I can change it or choose to continue what I do to him."* These people give themselves the power to control their own environment, which gives them more choices and helps them make better decisions. Which of the two are you?

3.   *"Can't you do anything RIGHT?"*

We really do take life way too seriously. For the sake of our children, we need to stop and remember how it felt when our parents were disappointed with us—unjustly. Being unreasonable and unfair defeats the whole purpose of being a parent. Our children need us to understand where we're coming from. When in doubt with what to do—be fair. Getting angry is okay, so long as it is for the *right* reason. If anger is only a means of lashing out or venting frustrations—or worse—of *hurting*, we need to ask ourselves why we even bothered becoming parents at all. If we tell our children that they can't do anything right, we will create our own self-fulfilling prophecy. Dorothy L. Nolte[1] wrote a poem called *Children Learn What They Live.* She writes: If children live with criticism, they learn to condemn. If children live with ridicule, they learn to be shy. On the other hand she also states: If children live with tolerance, they learn to be patient. If children live with encouragement, they learn to be confident.

As you know, being a parent isn't always easy but the efforts in

---

[1] I found this poem in a book called *Chicken Soup for the Soul,* pp. 85-86.

the long run can be the most rewarding and challenging experiences you'll ever have. You just need to make the right choices. And if you find that maybe you got angry unjustly, it's not too late to admit it—professing that your anger was wrong or unjust can make a world of difference. This can accomplish two things. One, your children will realize that you aren't perfect—imagine that. The downside is you'll need to realize it too. Those who choose not to admit imperfection are not facing reality. You can't be Superman and Wonderwoman but, if you want to be a fictional character, you can be Kings and Queens of De-nial. No one can possibly be perfect, so stop trying. Help your children have a more accurate view of human nature: make mistakes.

Secondly, your children will feel that you've taken the time to acknowledge their pain. They might even feel a degree of understanding for you. (This helps develop empathy—something we can all benefit from.)

Stop, You're on Candid Camera!

We need to think before we speak to our children. Often words spew out of our mouth before we have an opportunity to realize what we have said. Think about how you would feel if you knew someone could be *the fly on the wall* and hear what you were saying to your child. Would you be embarrassed by what they heard?

There have been many times where I have thought to myself, *"I am so glad no one heard how stupid I just sounded."* I am not proud of that but I have definitely learned from this experience. We all say things in a fit of rage but we must continuously remind ourselves that what we say directly affects our children.

I Christen Thee...

Can you remember doing something wrong as a child and hearing your first and middle name bellowed out? *"CHRISTINA MARIE!!!"* I think I hated my full name until I was 23 years old—simple because every time I heard the combination—I knew I was in trouble. Why do parents bother christening and blessing their children with a beautiful middle name if all they intended to do with it—is use it in anger and make their children hate it?

Do parents thoughtfully choose names for their children to express how they feel about them, or do they chose the combination to use as a weapon? Parents who do this have taken this precious gift to their children and have made it a punishment. They make their children hate the very thing that they (the parent) once believed was beautiful. Would we like it if our boss yelled out our first and middle name every time she was not pleased with us?

Children's Anger

Now that I have simultaneously criticized and validated *our* anger, let's talk about our children's anger. Just like us, our children experience anger too—maybe perhaps even to a greater extent than we do because they have not developed the necessary coping skills to deal with their environment. As their frustration mounts their emotions will soar. There are two things we can do to help defuse this potential explosion of emotions.

One, we can recognize our child's unstable emotions before they escalate to an uncontrollable point. This can easily be accomplished by paying attention to the signals the child is emitting *then* responding sooner rather than later. We can look at their inability to deal with their frustrations as a small spark flickering: if water is thrown on it we immediately douse it, but if we overreact and throw kerosene on it, we have just ignited the spark and caused an uncontrollable forest fire.

We can also look at these emotions as a potential bomb that needs to be defused. The emotional bomb can be disabled by carefully recognizing and acknowledging their anger. Some parents tend to discount their children's feelings by making statements like:

> *"You don't really feel that way."*
> *"You have no reason to react like that."*
> *"What did you do to make your friend yell at you?"*
> *"Stop acting like a baby."*
> *"Shush...it's okay."*

These statements will only make the situation worse. Even the last statement, trying to dissuade the child that he is angry can have the effect of denying the child his anger. You must acknowledge that these feelings are *real* and let him know that you understand that. The anger belongs to your children and not to you. A simple *acknowledgement* can often smother the smoldering match and put out the potential fire.

An example of how this might play out:

"You must really feel angry right now because usually you don't speak to your brother like that."

"I can see that you are mad so perhaps later when you feel comfortable, we can talk about it. It's up to you, okay?"

Many times, the signal your child is sending means she just want you to know that something is wrong. She is saying:

"I feel invisible, so please see and hear my feelings. I want to know that I exist. If you think my feelings are unimportant, I must be unimportant too."

As children develop, their need for acknowledgement and validation will increase. Every day they are growing right in front of our eyes. The problem sometimes is that we forget to grow with them. We will continue to make choices for our children as though they were still two years old. We must be aware of the fact that they are developing their own spirit and that we cannot 'beat' our philosophies into them.

Someone once told me that every person he had ever met contributed to who he had become. That profound statement struck me. Looking back, I believe the same holds for all of us. Our children will be exposed to so many challenges and adversities. We cannot prove to them that we are right. Each individual experience will contribute to who our children become. We can offer them our gift of wisdom but we cannot make them internalize it.

We can establish what we feel is acceptable behavior and what is not. This will place boundaries on their anger; yet, give them the necessary outlet for expressing themselves. To establish limitations, we must make a predefined list of "cans" and "cannots."

For example, when she is angry:

It is acceptable to:

1. Hit your bed or a punching bag
2 Tear paper into pieces

3 Scream into a pillow
4. Talk about anger

It is not acceptable to:

1. Hit your brother
2. Destroy other people's property

3. Yell at your parents
4. Be obnoxious (however you define it)

I used this method to deal with my nephew's anger and it was working perfectly until...one day, he and I were driving down the road. I knew that he was angry but surprisingly his response was expressed with tears. I asked him why he was crying and he said that he was angry and there weren't any acceptable ways to express his anger in the car. There wasn't any paper to tear up and he didn't have a punching bag.

I immediately felt for him because I could appreciate his frustration. He was trying to do the right thing, but felt stuck. I told him that we would have to think of something that would give him the opportunity to vent his frustration in the car. We both laughed and moved on to something more significant, like what kind of ice cream we were going to get at the store.

What I am trying to say is this: Nothing but your love should be set in stone and there are always other alternatives to dealing with your children's reactions—as new ideas come up, just add them to the list.

If a child does begin to rant and rave—do not give in to the natural temptation to rant right back! I know that you are probably saying, *"Yeh, right!"* But if we really stop to think about it, we would realize that such a reaction on our part usually makes the situation more explosive. Instead, say something like this (calmly),

"I would really love to listen to you but my ears don't work very well with loud noises, if the noise was softer, I

Be patient. This will seem irritating at first but it works. Use high, cheerful tones when addressing children, they will react much more positively. Remember, attitudes are contagious. Let's spread some cheer. Since it is our responsibility as parents to set the tone in our household, let us move in a direction that is more positive and upbeat. If we want our children's behavior to change without using anger, we will have to work hard to not take their anger personally. We all get frustrated, but we have to remember that anger is often more destructive than constructive.

I used to get angry with my nephew because he would say that he hated everything I cooked before he had even tried it. Night after night, this went on, with me getting increasingly frustrated. I wondered how on earth I could make *this kid* stop doing this to me. Because, after all, my cooking really isn't that bad—honest.

I decided I was tired of being angry. I told him, *"From now on, if you say you don't like what I cook even before you taste it, we'll have it the next night for dinner."* Of course, he tested me on this—so I had to follow through on my threat. This method worked, I haven't had to get angry about dinner since. He might make a face every now and then, but he doesn't make any comments regarding my food. An important aspect of this is to administer the punishment *without* anger. If we are angry, our children will shut us out.

Recently, I found myself getting increasingly angry with Katlin and with more frequency about other behavioral issues and taking things too personally. Again I was frustrated with the fact that I was not in control—no matter how angry I got—I was getting nowhere fast. I began thinking about this chapter and decided that perhaps I just needed to chill out and become more consistent with my punishment (take my own advice).

What I have found is that following through with consequences (without anger) and not personalizing the child's behavior, helps alleviate some of the anger. Really our kids are not out to get us. They are just growing and trying to become their own selves.

Take the following steps to accomplish objectives without harming your child's self-esteem.

****Expressing Anger Constructively****
****Separating Behavior And Child****
****Following Through With Consequences****
****Releasing Anger Then Moving On****

Homework

Anger: Right or Responsibility?

A lot of our frustration is due to the fact that we haven't given ourselves enough time to relax. We need to be calm in order to practice good parenting. You will be amazed how much difference a few minutes alone can make. For this exercise, make fifteen minutes where there are no distractions.

Get into a comfortable position. Close your eyes. Next, listen to and concentrate on your breathing. Inhale through your nose and exhale through your month. Concentrate on a word, like train, flower or any word you choose. As you breathe out, think of that word. This helps release your thoughts from the day.

This exercise may be more difficult than you think, but the more you practice, the better you will become. And as you get better, you will experience the benefit of it. This exercise will best serve you if you find you are getting upset with your children more than you feel is appropriate.

Now that you have finished this part of the exercise, think about a situation in which you got angry with your child. See whether there have been any alternative approaches to dealing with the situation.

Journal Notes

CHAPTER SIX

"DO AS I SAY, NOT AS I DO"

"Do As I Say, Not As I Do"

Setting an Example for Children

We have all heard this line, or some variation of it, at one time in our lives. This is one of the least effective means of teaching a child to *internalize* right from wrong. The only time (and I say this with great conviction) that this phrase is truly useful is if your intent is to alienate yourself from your children. What you are teaching them (role-modeling) is, *"just don't do this until you grow up."* They won't internalize right from wrong. As they become older, their image of you will gradually shift toward one of separateness. The growing process pushes children to seek autonomy from their parents. They want to separate themselves and become their "own" person.

When a parent practices the do-as-I-say concept a child eventually concludes that this parent is one who talks out of both sides of his mouth. Each time these thoughts of hypocrisy are validated, it reaffirms the child's conclusion about the parent. Then a snowball effect makes the child quickly lose respect for who that parent is and what he stands for.

Generally speaking, most people like to understand why they are required to do certain tasks, and children are no exception. When possible, a parent should afford his kids this same privilege: attach an explanation to the demand. Explanations will do two things: (1) they will make the parent determine whether the request is valid enough, and (2) they will provide an environment for the children that promotes better judgment. When children have more information they can make better choices.

As a child matures, she learns that some things cannot always be taken at face value. She will learn to separate truths from untruths as she learns good judgment. It's doing our kids a great disservice when we try to force them to accept everything they hear from adults.

We've all experienced a time when we're asked to do something that we felt wasn't necessary. We had to decide whether we wanted to do what we were *told* or whether we wanted to question authority. It's important to teach children to challenge things that don't *feel* right. This will not only teach them good judgment, it will also teach them how to protect themselves against bad adults who misuse their positions of authority. If *we* don't accept everything we hear from others as gospel, should we expect children to accept what they are told as absolute?

When children understand 'why' something must be done, it's easier for them to swallow. There are, of course, exceptions to every rule, but as a general practice—let them know the reason. This gives them a CHANCE to accept and internalize the rules more easily.

Respect

Respect: n. 1. The state of being regarded with honor or esteem, or the willingness to show consideration or appreciation.[1]

Consideration for children's feelings is often one of the most overlooked mistakes that I see parents make. Many believe respect is something that should be earned over a long period of time. Consequently, many adults do not view children with the level of respect they might deserve—simply because they *lack* experience. When adults repeat the phrase, *"Do as I say and not as I do,"* they are conditioning their children to believe that they are unworthy of respect and honor. When children hear this phrase they begin to internalize the message and accept it as truth. The following are some examples of *how* a child may interpret the message:

"I know there are rules, but they only apply to you."
"You must respect me, but I don't need to respect you."
"How I feel is important, but what you feel is not."
"I am someone, but you are not."

Can you hear the same sense of unfairness that I do? Does this sound like a set of rules that you could live by? If you are a parent who believes in the do-as-I-say concept, would you say that this philosophy works well for you? If rules *only* apply to children, then at what age do you initiate regard for them as individuals and give

---

[1] American Heritage Dictionary, 2nd Edition, 1985.

them the right to express their own identity? Is this a rite of passage that is bestowed upon individuals because they *deserve* it, or simply because they have made it to adulthood?

We all want to feel that others in our lives love and respect us. We need to know that the efforts we're making mean something and that we aren't taken for granted. We desire acknowledgment, whether it be in our jobs or with our family and friends. Now—is there any reason to assume that these needs are exclusive to adults? At what point do we earn the right to have such needs and desires for acknowledgment? This question cannot be answered for the simple reason that those needs are already there, in every individual, from the very beginning. As an adult, you have a need to be understood and respected. Your child has an equal need—and that understanding and respect is needed most significantly from you.

Professionals believe that nurturing and promoting regard for children should begin early to help them grow up healthy and happy. We all want to be good parents. But can we honestly say we respect our children? Do we "regard them with honor?" Do we value them as the people that they are? Many parents simply overlook respect as an option for their children. After all, they're just kids, right?

It is vital that you hear and value your children as the people that they are, in order to help them become the adults they need to be. Think about this the next time your reflex is to take the do-as-I-say approach. Ask yourself whether or not you truly regard your children with the *"respect and esteem"* they deserve.

Until recently, the philosophy has always been that children should be seen and not heard. Changing this concept means changing an entire mind-set (a very major task). Such a change, to say the least, can be a slow process, requiring commitment, time and focus to make the difference. The good news is, if you've got the commitment, the time and focus will follow.

Recall for a moment when you were a child—who always had to sit at the small card table during holiday dinners? Do you remember ever seeing your father sit in the back seat of the car while you rode up front? Were you permitted to tell your parents not to interrupt while you were talking on the phone? Why was that the case? When children are forced to "respect" others without receiving reciprocity, what is it that they really learn? Maybe that others are worthy of respect and they are not?

As mentioned in Chapter 3, it is easier to build a child rather than to repair an adult. Do we wait until the damage is done and try to repair it later...or do we give our kids a CHANCE and help them love themselves, now? The key is to use a proactive attitude.

Alarmingly, many adults suffer from a low self-worth. Why is that? My guess is, they were *seen and not heard.*

"I see you but, I don't want to hear you. I don't hear you because what you have to say is not important. Because what you say is not important, you too must not be important."

Childhood is one long—often painful—learning process. It is a time of learning one's identity. Everything you learn in childhood is transferable to adulthood. It's either heavy baggage to be shlepped through life, or it's money in the bank. It's largely our choice as parents which of those two will be the case for our children.

The Referee Calls "Time-Out"

Watching a football game, you see the team captain gesture for a time-out because the other team is gaining. You hear the ref call, "time-out!" Then all the team members huddle together and discuss strategies. When you think of a time-out during a game, do you think of it in terms of punishing the team for screwing up? Or is it perhaps a moment for the team to give themselves an opportunity to regroup? The answer, of course, is the latter.

The concept of "time-out" for children was originally created for the same purpose: to give them a break and help everyone regroup. It was set up to give children time to find positive ways to change behavior.

Recently, I've noticed that many people have sort of twisted the concept of time-out for their children, using it as a punishment. Time-out was never intended to be punitive. It was intended to give kids a CHANCE to redirect their behavior and get more effective results. This time away is a help for children—and for parents as well. In a fit of rage, parents may say or do things that they wished they had not—often taking a superior stance and not permitting the child to defend himself (do-as-I-say...). It is far easier to hold back hurtful words—if you give yourself a CHANCE to regroup via "time-out"—than it is to take those hurtful words back.

Try to think like referees and call time-out the *right* way. Remember that the time-out concept can be applied to yourself as well—do not restrict it solely to your children. You may find that you were wrong. If you can accept that time-out is a positive experience, you will see amazing results. Once again, however, you must keep in mind that parenting is not easy and that this, like everything else, will take a lot of practice. But it is well worth it.

Rules for Time-Out

1. <u>Attitude</u>: It is extremely important that anger is not present when administering time-out (TO). We might want to be angry but, if we really want effective TO then we cannot show it. Remember, we are trying to change the behavior. We should try to keep in mind that it is the *behavior* that we are unhappy with, not the child.

2. Duration: One minute for each year of the child's age should be the maximum used for TO. If the child is two then only place him in TO for two minutes. The reasoning is that if he sits too long, he will forget why he is there. Then the time-out has been rendered useless. Besides, have you ever seen a coach place her team in a TO for two hours? The team's momentum would be lost; like your child, they may not feel motivated to learn from their mistakes.

3. Application: When the time-out is up—go to the child. Get down on his level and make eye contact, then talk to him about the behavior in a gentle and loving way (this is a lot easier said than done—but possible). Talk about choices and options and the importance of making the right decision. *Most importantly*, make him understand it is the *behavior* that you do not like and not him. Give him a hug and tell him that you love him. This may seem foreign, because most people do not remember punishment being positive. But it does work if the procedure is done correctly.

4. Ownership: When you find that *you* are the one with the undesirable behavior, give yourself a time-out. When you are more calm—talk out the problem. There really is no benefit to reaching solutions when you are out of control with anger.

Removal of Privileges

Removal of privileges is another way to get effective results. For example, if your child receives an allowance (privilege), you can reduce it. Begin by setting an amount for the allowance. Next, make a list of behaviors that need to be changed then assign each behavior a fine. For example, if the child leaves toys laying around, she loses five cents. Talking back, inappropriately, 15 cents. Not listening, ten cents and so on. If she depend on that allowance, she will not want to lose it. This is my version of Shock Therapy and if it is administered properly, it *will* work. I would caution you though that if the penalty is too stiff and she loses her entire allowance, she'll perceive this as failure rather than success. Research has shown that when a child fails too often, she will stop trying and your efforts will be lost. The failure is referred to as learned helplessness.

To counteract some of the penalties, you can use an intermittent reward system to compensate for too many failures. When a child loses too much of her allowance, acknowledge a good behavior and give her a *bonus.* This will reinforce winning and serve as a great motivational factor.

Role Modeling

When I taught Head Start, I took my class on a field trip to the police station. One of the boys was watching a police officer demonstrate the alcohol breath-a-lizer test. He interrupted, *"Hey my dad drinks beer!"* The police officer said, *"Well, Steven, that's okay so long as he doesn't drink while he's driving."* Steven's reply was, *"My dad has one hand on the steering wheel and one hand on a beer—he does it all the time."* The police officer said, *"Steven isn't your dad's name...?"*

The issue here is that our children see what is going on around them. We might want to believe that they are too young to understand, but the fact is they understand much more than we give them credit for. Children are more sensitive to their environment than we are (we have all heard children referred to as sponges that soak up everything around them). They know when there are problems—although no words are spoken they *feel* that something is wrong. If we underestimate their ability to see our problem, then we are only fooling ourselves.

If there are conflicts at home, I guarantee that the children are involved. They are exposed to all of our disagreements whether they are an active participant or not. I knew a woman who described her husband's abusive behavior to her mother-in-law and the mother looked at her as though she knew this deep dark secret about her. This woman asked her what was wrong and she said, *"My ex-*

husband would do the exact same things to me. But I never let the children see." The fact is, they do see, hear, and internalize everything you do and they learn by example. The reality is that they will learn, most specifically, from your example how to behave—regardless of your intent. Role-modeling is just too powerful. Consequently, can you really expect children to only do as you say and not as you do?

Raise With Praise

The world is a complicated place. There is so much to do and accomplish. Parents can get caught up in all the shoulds and should nots and it becomes easy to focus on the negative.

"Why didn't you finish your homework?"
"Why is your room dirty?"

Negative forces, if permitted, can consume our children's lives. We need to find ways to counteract some of these negatives.

One way is to use praise whenever we possibly can. Some parents may overlook praise as an option—simply because they believe a child *should* just behave himself (without any recognition). *"Why should I tell him that I am proud of him for not hitting his sister—he just shouldn't do that."* Ask yourself each time you think that your child doesn't deserve praise what it would hurt to say something good. Does it hurt to say to him that you are proud of his behavior? When your child continuously hears praise, he will eventually learn to view himself more positively; with hope, he will develop the ability to praise himself. Not only will a child gain a positive outlook, he will feel a sense of accomplishment which will in turn reinforce good feelings. Show him through your own behavior that you are positive and he will be positive.

As a home-based teacher, I would put smiley stickers on children's paper when they did good work. *"Boy, you really really deserve that smiley face. This is the greatest picture I have ever seen. Look mom (referring to child's mother), see how great he did."* Then one day, a student of mine made a picture for me and she pasted a smiley face in the corner. I commented on how beautiful the picture was and how great the smiley face looked on the picture. Her reply was, *"Well, I did such a great job."* That kind of attitude will last a lifetime and give her the best CHANCE in life to excel.

"Model high standards and children will strive for excellence."[2]

---

[2] I wrote this down in my notes during an early child education class ten years ago.

Tools for building

Very often people act out of habit, with no particularly good reason for that habit. What parents need to do is build a new paradigm—change how to think and see things. The following story illustrates this point. A husband asked his wife. *"Honey, why do you cut both ends of the fish off before you fry it?"* She replied, *"I don't*

know, my mother always did it, why don't you ask her?" So he asked his mother-in-law, *"Why do you cut both ends of the fish off before you fry it?"* She replied, *"I don't know, my mother always did it, why don't you ask her?"* Then the young man went to the grandmother and asked, *"Why do you cut both ends of the fish off before you fry it?"* She replied, measuring with her hands, *"Because the fish is this big, and my pan is only this big."*

The point is, what we have learned and made habit may not apply to our situation at all. And that can set us up for parenting problems. We learn a great deal through observation, and often we are unconsciously emulating our parents' behavior without fully understanding why. We need to take a better look at what we are presenting to our children. We need to make a conscious decision as to whether the things we have learned from our parents are the same things we want to teach our children. Finding the right parenting tools will make our children have a greater sense of self-worth.

By giving our children a CHANCE to love themselves, we are instilling a gift called quality. We will have to change how we nurture their egos. This may seem difficult at first, but once we get the hang of it...we will be well on our way.

Let's begin by examining ineffective parenting tools. For instance, do you know parents who use the same form of punishment over and over again, even when it isn't working? Parents who continue to use ineffective tools cannot reach resolution. Ironically, these tools are probably the only tools they will continue to use. For example, if you know that a wrench is too small, do you continue to try and use it? Of course not. What do you do?—Right, you get a different one. Why? Because the wrench is too small and it doesn't work. If you have a frying pan that always makes food stick. Would you use it to prepare a meal for your company dinner party? Probably not. Why? Because it doesn't work. If it makes so much sense to change these inadequate tools, then why do parents continually use the same methods of punishment on their children when they know the punishment doesn't work?

We have all heard this:

"I have screamed at her a million times and she still hasn't done what I've told her."

"I have grounded him 6,000 times and he still won't make his bed."

Well obviously, this isn't working. Think of something new and different that you can do—change the old parenting tools in order to get your kids to listen to what you are saying. Of course, everyone understands that changing parenting tools is not so easy as finding a new wrench. But it can—and should—be done.

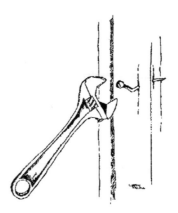

"The Wrong Tool"

Options which get results

1. <u>Reward system:</u> Find something that your child would enjoy doing and set up a *reward system.* Examples might be a movie, a favorite meal, or a ball game. We do these things with our kids anyway—why not have them earn it? Believe it or not children like earning privileges. Subconsciously, they want structure and, most importantly, they need it. It might not be fun or easy for them (or you) at first, but they'll catch on and so will you. Earning the privilege also gives them a sense of accomplishment and ultimately gives them the power of achievement.

2. <u>Eye Contact:</u> How many of us yell at our kids from across the room? Do we really think that they hear us? Of course they don't. There may be several reasons, such as the child is tuning out what he doesn't want to hear. But even this can be overcome by making *eye-to-eye contact.* To get a child's attention, we must kneel down and look him straight in the eye. It is amazing how much more effective parenting will be, not to mention the amount of time we will save.

3. <u>Slow down:</u> Sometimes we think, *"Who has time for all of this?"* Between the job, housework, soccer practice and everything else—where will we find time for learning these new tools? The answer is *slow down.* As hard as that may seem, if we do not rearrange our priorities nothing will change. We have to slow down and make some choices. If our lives are too chaotic it is impossible to coordinate

anything. Decide what is more important, and the time will follow. Time is like money—we spend what we make. Prioritizing can help the chaos become more manageable.

4. <u>Time Management.</u> Closely related to #3 is *time management.* Using time management more effectively will be a great tool for better parenting. In Stephen R. Covey's book, *The 7 Habits of Highly Effective People,* he suggests to his readers that it is important to stop for a moment and sharpen the saw (his 7th habit). He talks about a man who was feverishly sawing down a tree for over five hours. When the man was asked to take a break and sharpen the saw, he replied, *"I don't have time—I'm too busy."* To be the most effective parent, stop and think how much time you could save by sharpening this very important parenting tool. Parents need to work smarter, not harder.

Scenario

Here is a situation that has two seemingly contradictory objectives (child and parent). What is the solution?

Child: Your child wants to finish painting a picture that she has been working on.

Parent: You want to have dinner early in order to sit down and relax.

Neither of you can give in unless a compromise has truly been made and you both win. But how can this be a win-win situation?

A solution:

1. Get eye contact.

2. Prepare the child and tell her in advance that dinner will be early tonight. *"Dinner will be ready in 30 minutes. Okay Susie...Dinner will be ready in 15 minutes...Get ready for dinner in 5 minutes and so on."* Always get a response by saying *"Okay Susie?"* That makes the child feel as though she is a part of the decision making process and she can manage her time more effectively. You prepared her in advance and she understood what you expected from her. This goes back to simply respecting and validating a child's sense of self-worth.

3. Then reinforce the compliance. *"I really do appreciate it when you are such a great listener. It really makes me feel good that you are such a big girl."* Then do something for the child later in the evening to reinforce behavior: *"Susie, since you were such a great listener today I'll let you choose the TV program tonight, or you can have your choice of snack."*

Some parents are saying, *"Hey, I am the boss and she should just do as she's told."* Well, the fact is parents *are* the boss, *but* how effective are they? Are their objectives being met with little to no effort? If the answer is "yes" then the parents are on the right track. If the answer is "no" then these parents need to use a different wrench or frying pan.

Can you use the new tool once and see instant behavioral

changes? Probably not. A child's first reaction is confusion: *"What are my parents doing? They have never treated me like this before."* The novelty of your 'new attitude' may be followed by some sort of manipulation. *"Since they are in such a good mood, I might as well take full advantage."* Children are opportunists. If they say something like, *"I did what you told me...now can I have one more piece of candy?"* You could respond by saying something like, *"I'm really glad you listened to me and I know how much you LOVE candy, but it's almost time for dinner. Why don't we talk about this later? You have been a great listener so I want to make sure that you are rewarded, Okay?"* You were able to get them to do what you wanted and they felt like you understood. You will need to reinforce this with *consistency.*

Consistency with children is probably the hardest behavior for adults to change. For most of us, we do not feel that we have the *time* or the *energy* to be consistent. And generally, consistency is more painful for the adult than for the child. We have all heard this: *"This is gonna hurt me a lot more than it is gonna hurt you."* And there is some truth to that statement.

An example: I was having difficulty with my nephew using inappropriate ways to express his anger. I tried many alternatives to stop the behavior, but nothing was successful. One day, I told him that I would take away his roller skating privilege (one of the activities most precious to him) if he chose to use inappropriate means to express his anger.

As difficult as it was for me, the time came and I had to follow through. Needless to say he wasn't the only one surprised or hurt by this need for consistency. A good friend of his was meeting him at the skating rink and he pleaded with me to take away all of his other privileges anything but roller skating. He desperately pleaded, *"Please... You can take away my privileges for the next year, but not this time. You can even take away my privilege to open my Christmas presents on Christmas morning, but please don't take away my privilege today."* I said to him that this skating day must be really important and that I was sorry; but unfortunately, there are consequences to bad behavior. I wanted with the same desperation to believe him when he said that he would never do it again. But, if I didn't follow through with my threat to take the privilege, he would not take me seriously the next time I threatened him. My only option was to follow through. Result—I felt like *crap* all morning. Out of sheer agony, I called the babysitter and asked how he had taken not getting to roller skate. She said he was fine. It appears that I am the one who suffered the most. Children *want* and *need* consistency, whether it feels good at the time or not. They need to know they can count on us.

Of all the techniques, or tools, we've discussed in this chapter, consistency is the most important. If you put your efforts most into consistency the other tools will be easier to obtain. Just remember, what you are doing says a lot to your kids. Therefore, have them do as you say and as *you* do!

Homework

Do As I Say, Not As I Do

This homework assignment will be to learn as much about your children's personality as you can and learn to respect them for the individuals that they are. The goal is to find as many things as you can. For a period of one week, write down everything that you learn about your child. Find out the answers by making a statement about yourself—first. Example could be: *"I really love blue—do you? I think blue is my favorite color. What is your favorite color? How many blue toys do you have?"* You will be amazed at how much conversation that you can create and how much they want to be like you.

Find your child's:

1. Favorite color   _____
2. Favorite sport   _____
3. Best friend   _____
4. Favorite teacher   _____
5. Best subject in school   _____
6. Favorite foods   _____
7. Best television show   _____
8. Favorite past time   _____
9. Favorite animal   _____
10. Favorite toy and why   _____
11. Add your own category_____

Journal Notes

CHAPTER SEVEN

TOTAL QUALITY
PARENTING (TQP)

Total Quality Parenting

Being the best that you can be!

Today, throughout America, corporations are using a relatively new technique referred to as Total Quality Management (TQM). This innovative method of management has improved interaction between management and its staff. TQM focuses on the importance of addressing an employee's individual needs, then following through with a plan to reach a comparable resolution to that employee's issues. When TQM is applied properly, there are significant increases in productivity and an overall improvement in morale.

The basic TQM philosophy is mutual respect with regard for individuals and their differences. If this technique can be successfully incorporated into the business world, then there is a good CHANCE it can successfully work in the parenting world—where "management" and "staff" crises occur all the time.

This chapter focuses on how you can apply new techniques to your current parenting styles, in order to arrive at Total Quality Parenting (TQP). You learned about regard and respect in chapter 6, *Do As I Say, Not As I Do.* This chapter lets you use what you've learned there and move forward!

A Parent's Position of Authority

Essentially your position in the home can be defined as manager, production supervisor, Human Resource Officer, liaison plus so much more. As parenting director for this not-for-profit group, you'll need to establish TQP skills that will benefit your staff yet yield results that make them want to work *with* rather than *against* you.

Each TQP program will depend on the philosophy of the family and its different personalities. This makes each program special. Essentially, you must develop a business plan for your family, then implement the procedures according to your *designed doctrines*. The *plan* will act as your outline. As new ideas and methods prove successful, add them to your plan. Sit down and have meetings with your kids and find out how they feel.

Because all children are unique, there isn't any hard and fast methodology that can be applied universally. Be flexible and unconventional—find what motivates them and apply it. Run your family like an office and use a new style to work with your kids.

A business manager who transfers to a new company, for example, must use flexibility and open-mindedness in her approach toward her new employee personalities. Take for instance, the techniques that are applicable to autoworkers, probably won't work so well for secretaries. Likewise, in parenting, each individual child must be assessed and a plan created separately to meet his needs.

As mentioned above, children possess many differences and some parenting styles might need alterations to enhance the effects of TQP. There isn't anything necessarily wrong with your (unusual) child, he's just different. Although there are differences in all children, there are also many similarities that we can rely on. Their basic needs—love, attention, self-regard etc.—are some of those similarities that we can count on. They can serve as part of your baseline for your organizational plan. Based upon these similarities, you can establish some guidelines to create a foundation for new and improved parenting.

Plan to Prevent

Part of your plan needs to include prevention. This is two thirds of the parenting game. Incorporating prevention into your new plan will provide a more conducive environment for parenting. When you can anticipate (prevention planning) a child's feelings, it will be easier to intercept undesirable behavior *before* it occurs. Use chapter 4, *"Hey, I'm Talking to You,"* and recall some points regarding body language to help with prevention.

Body language helps a parent understand what a child is trying to say through her movements when she cannot find the words verbally to express herself. This will be crucial when trying to determine how to combat her undesirable behavior. Some behaviors that you want to 'plan to prevent' will be fear, anxiety, frustration, surprise and disappointment. (I'm not asking for much!)

Children have a difficult time coping with their emotions, particularly negative ones. As mentioned in Chapter 4, most don't possess the adequate language skills required to express themselves. Children frequently mishandle their emotions, which creates problems that are manifested as 'undesirable behavior.' Consequently, children often express their emotions inappropriately through anger.

A child can display emotions that may "appear" angry, when in actuality what the parent sees is the result of a lack of knowledge. You need to stop and assess what your child is really feeling. If you can head her off at the pass, you can eliminate a great deal of the undesired behavior without the child even knowing what hit her.

Living with a child day-in and day-out, gives you the ability to predict, to some degree, how he will react to a particular situation. For instance, you may always have problems with Tommy at bed time. He cries and whines about not being tired, he's thirsty, or he's afraid of being alone. You know exactly what game he's playing. Now all you have to do is figure out how to combat it.

The goal is to get this kid into bed and try to enjoy five minutes of peace and quiet before you drop from exhaustion. Ideally, you want to accomplish this without the manipulation and power struggle. The problem is that the timing stinks. Your energy reserve and tolerance level are low.

There are a few options which you can choose. You can rant, scream, and turn blue in the face...or you can use TQP. Using Total Quality Parenting, you can analyze "why" Tommy is reacting so strongly and develop new methods to fix the problem. Once you assess why Tommy doesn't want to go to bed, work on a plan to change these feelings and make the night time ritual more appealing, thereby planning to prevent.

What most parents have done (without perhaps realizing it) is made bed time a punishment. Children have concluded that bed is something *negative* and should be avoided at all cost. Parents have all at one time or another threatened children with something like this:

"If you don't behave yourself, I will send you to bed."

"All right young lady, march your little buns into bed for that one."

Does this sound familiar? Parents have conditioned their children to equate bad behavior with bed. Even when bed is not a punishment, the child may view it as such.

Bed ≈ Bad

When children anticipate that an event is undesirable, they will react adversely to it (like going to bed). This sort of situation causes parents to lash back and overreact. Using bed time as a punishment makes *"going to your room"* a bad experience.

"Just go to bed and quit giving me so much lip."

"If you can't listen to me without an argument, just go to your room."

There are things that can be done to change your child's opinion of bed time if you just think TQP. Start by finding what makes your child tick (meaning what motivates him) then using those incentives to get results rather than punishing him with bed. Take bed time and turn it into something fun and positive. For example, you can prepare your child for bed by spending time with him in his room (for at least thirty minutes) prior to bed time. Ideally, some time would actually be spent in the bed so that he sees that bed is not so bad. You can read him a book, sing him a song or just tell him a story.

My nephew and I like to go on imagery trips that we call journeys. While he is tucked in bed I have him close his eyes and we begin our journeys. We will go under the ocean, riding on the back of a killer whale; we will ride through the sky on a Pegasus horse; or we will wander through the desert looking for snakes and reptiles.

And amazingly enough, sometimes the journeys knock him out. There are even times when my stories are so good that they knock me out too!

This is a particularly fun exercise for many reasons. It helps promote creativity and imagination: it provides children with a new coping skill (relaxation), and you can expand on this game by looking for things in your *real* environment that can be used to help expand the journeys.

My nephew and I will be driving down the road and see a cloud that is special then I will say, *"Remember this cloud and we can use it in our next journey."* This helps your children become aware of their environment which may help them later remember to stop and smell the roses. This is something parents sometimes forget.

An imagination has the potential to change your entire outlook. Focusing on the good things will help you develop greater TQP skills and make your job as parent a little easier. This was only one example of how to make bed time more fun. Be creative and look for things that will make your kids want to be there.

Another part of TQP is not becoming a fortune teller or mind reader. Often, this practice breaks down communication. Children feel misunderstood and resentful. Always ask your children how they feel, don't assume that you know. We've all heard our parents say, *"One of these days you are gonna..."* Percentage-wise parents are often wrong, but when they're right, they'll let you know it! A parent who is a fortune teller and forecasts long enough, eventually they're going to be right (it is just a matter of time).

Once as young adults, my mother's fortune telling came true. My sister and I would drive to her house in our pajamas in the early evening to visit her. She would always say, *"You girls are gonna be sorry—one of these days..."* I guess my sister and I commuted in our jammies for two months to our mothers house (thinking it was cute to irritate her). Then one night my sister's car over heated in the middle of town. A white cloud was spewing out of the engine. My sister got out and started running around the car screaming, *"The car's on fire, the car's on fire."* Being 17, I decided it would be less painful to blow up with the car than to be seen in my pajamas. Guess what my mother said!

We lost that time to fortune telling due to the odds. But, the fact is if we'd only done it once, she would have been wrong, but we *had to* push it (being a teen requires this defiance). To a kid there isn't anything worse than hearing a parent say, *"I told you so."* Children don't appreciate fortune telling—no matter how good the intentions. I remember rolling my eyes every time my mother said anything like that to me. Now, as adults, my sister and I can look back and understand why she said the things she did. Yet, I know that, at the time, the approach seemed all wrong. The good news is, this experience became a great memory—we still laugh about it to this day.

One thing I've learned from being a parent is, no matter how hard we work or how conscientious we become...we're going to screw up. Being a parent requires a lot of effort and we can't always be on top of things. But we can use our new management styles to show our kids that we care and respect how they feel.

A good strategy is to start each day over—like it was your first. Hopefully, you can learn from each mistake made the day before. Don't be so hard on yourself when you do make mistakes. Consider failure as just another opportunity to start over. You'll be surprised with the results. Kids are resilient and can bounce back from a bad day much easier than you can. They are much more forgiving too when they get an apology. If you mess up, your kids will still love you. A friend of mine once enrolled in a child psychology class, she came to me very upset, *"Oh Christina, I did everything wrong."*

Obviously this mother overreacted (because I know her kids and they're just fine), but it doesn't take away the guilt a parent carries for making mistakes. Know that you're doing the best you can. The fact that you bought a parenting book shows that you want to be the best parent that you can be. My belief is that as long as you give it an honest effort, your children will turn out okay. Like I've said before, it's never too late (the parental bond with your children lasts a lifetime).

When we dreamed of becoming parents, most of us never envisioned the reality to be this difficult. I know that I sometimes feel alone and it is overwhelming to realize that I am holding a child's life in my hands—he depends on and needs me. As I've made mistakes, I've tried to learn from them. I too have read my share of parenting books: some were very funny, others were stupid and many were just plain unrealistic. But from each book I've learned something valuable, that is, to be persistent and always being willing to try new things.

I would encourage you to evaluate each technique that you have learned and give it serious consideration before you implement it. Apply the ones that you think have potential and disregard the rest. I interpreted one book that I read as saying that if I followed the book's techniques my parenting problems would be over. I will caution you that this is not the case. Everyone is different; consequently, not all methods will work for everyone. You can decide what methods are best for you and your child. Trust your instincts.

Another problem I see is the misconception that any child can be perfect. A child who does not fail—*does not grow*. Let's make failure something positive. For if we continually remind our children that failure is bad, they will give up and stop trying.

As a psychology major, one thing I've learned is that we bring to parenting every perception we've experienced as children. The memories act as ghosts under our beds. Although we do not necessarily live with these ghosts everyday, external events can spark these memories and cause the ghosts to come out and haunt us.

As a child my ghost was losing a special treat. I loved eating peanut butter with a spoon. One day my new step-father decided that peanut butter should only be eaten on bread. I can remember how upset I was that this privilege was taken from me. Then one day (as an adult) my nephew asked me if he could eat some peanut butter with his fork.

At that moment, I felt this overwhelming sadness come over me. I told him (with conviction) that he could eat as much peanut butter as he wanted, any way he wanted. I felt vindicated. The problem is, my nephew never experienced the pain that I did. Consequently, this experience meant nothing significant to him, yet meant everything to me. He will not grow up and brag that he got to eat peanut butter with a fork. He will never understand nor appreciate what I had felt, and there will be times when he will experience pain that I will never be aware of.

What I want everyone to understand is that our children are not us. Do not bequeath the ghosts of *our* past to them. Childhood today is difficult enough without complicating it with all of our neuroses. Give them a CHANCE to live their own lives—they'll thank us later.

The 3rd Person Syndrome

A phenomenon that I find amazing is, what I call, the third person syndrome. This is when a parent talks to her child like she is another person. Why do we do this?

Mom: *"Jason, mommy's very tired, can you leave her alone?"*

I bet we have all done this. But why? If you think about it, it sounds pretty silly. Would you talk to a grown adult like this? Let's set up a scenario. You need to tell your boss that you cannot complete the report she asked for by the deadline.

Stephanie: *"Miss Davis, Stephanie was unable to complete the report on time, would you like her to work late?"*

An innocent by-stander may conclude that you suffer from delusional tendencies and may not want to associate with you. Your behavior will probably eliminate you from earning that big promotion into top management. The problem with the 3rd person syndrome is your children are not learning how to see you as a person. Your communication suggests to them that you are talking about someone who does not exist. If you want them to understand and respect you as a parent and manager, talk to them about who you are and how you feel. This will enhance your Total Quality Parenting.

TQP is something you need to continually maintain in order to be the best parent that you can be. Your children need you to show them that you appreciate their feelings. When they understand that you genuinely care, they will work harder to please you. Always think, Total Quality Parenting!

Homework

TQP

This assignment will help involve your children with family tasks, which will teach children more about responsibility. It will also give the family a CHANCE to improve communication and enhance quality time.

Together, prepare a menu for the entire week for all breakfasts and dinners. Ensure that the menus contain preparations that will include your children. As you can image, it will take longer to prepare the meals, but the goal here is to be a more interactive parent and, not to make "fast food." If you want fast food go to McDonalds.

Kids can help by cracking eggs (have them break them in separate bowl), crumbling bread (for stuffing or meatloaf), adding seasonings, cleaning vegetables etc. Note, only permit your child to do things that are age-appropriate (i.e. a two-year-old should stay away from the stove). Just use common sense. Let him do the *little things*—that will make him feel important.

Making dinner can be lots of fun. When you include your child, you are building confidence and self-worth. One thing to remember is to make recipes that will promote success. Do not be a gourmet chef right away—that comes with time. Also make sure that the child's preparation time does not exceed more than 15 minutes. His attention span might be short given his age. You may find that this time also improves the quality time that you are missing while you are in the kitchen and your child is in front of the television. The following page has a one week day-timer. Use this to record your meals.

Day	Breakfast	Dinner
Monday		
Tuesday		
Wednesday		
Thursday		
Friday		
Saturday		
Sunday		

Homework

TQP

We all have hectic and busy lives—work never seems to be done. Consequently, we get overwhelmed and feel guilty because we are letting things slide. This is probably the number one reason why most of us procrastinate. The more we procrastinate, the less enthusiastic we are, which creates more guilt. Get the picture? It becomes a vicious cycle.

Before you begin this second homework assignment, be sure that you have completed the first. Now that you understand what is more important, you need to learn how to prioritize and delegate tasks in order to minimize guilt.

First decide what are the most important tasks that need to be accomplished then evaluate how much time it will take to accomplish each one. If there are too many items on the list—it is time to DELEGATE. For the following assignment, write a list of tasks then number each one in order of importance then place a check mark by items that can be accomplished by someone else.

For those who live by the song, *"Nobody Does It Better"*—you are just fooling yourself—delegate...delegate...delegate...or experience parental burnout. I do not recommend the latter.

Remember to only number the items that you can get completed in one day. If you are an out-of-the-home working parent reduce your list to reflect the difference. We need to keep the rest of the time open for our children. Example:

_3_	Grocery store	1.0 hours
_5_	Laundry	2.5 hours
_2_	Income Tax Return	4.0 hours
_1_	Mortgage payment	0.5 hours √
_4_	Clean up the yard	2.5 hours √
TOTAL		10.5 hours
Amount of time that you have		7.5 hours
Time to Delegate		(3.0) hours

It doesn't matter who you designate to do what is left but it is important that you accomplish what you *need* to do. If your expectations are met, this will reduce your guilt and help you feel a sense of accomplishment. This in turn will give you a better attitude and give you permission to enjoy your children.

Not only are you respecting your child but you are incorporating good time management. Remember, your child is used to a different method of parenting, so it may take some time—don't give up. Write down the results after each time you attempt to prepare your child. Gradually, you should see a difference.

Journal Notes

CHAPTER EIGHT

BM HELPS REGULARITY

BM Helps Regularity

Consistency is the key!

No—BM stands for *Behavior Modification*. (Good thing this is the final chapter. Everyone's mind including my own has hit bottom, no pun intended.) Anyway, back to my final words.

As mentioned throughout this book, behavior modification takes time and a great deal of energy. Modification entails practicing new behaviors with *consistency* while simultaneously becoming conscious enough to 'unlearn' old patterns with the same amount of *regularity*.

Setting new standards for children and ourselves will be an arduous task—but a necessary one. Much of this book has discussed changing behavior. Yet we haven't focuses specifically on learning modification techniques. Applying more positive techniques will improve behaviors that are most desirable and minimize the ones that aren't so great. Many experts believe that behaviors are learned through a series of trials and errors (reaction to the environment). Children learn that a particular behavior can elicit a particular response (much like Pavlov's dogs).

Modification, according to the New World Dictionary, refers to a partial or slight change in form or a change in an organism caused by its environment and not inheritable. Although there are some personality traits children possess inherently, children learn many things from their surroundings.

What do you do for children for whom tried and true techniques do not work? Throw convention out the window and start fresh. Having certain predispositions only means that children need us to find a different way to parent.

Each person learns differently: some learn by reading...others learn by doing. Children aren't any different than that except for the fact that they lack experience to deal with their feelings. They are inherently good and want to do what's right. We just need to find alternatives to behavior that make them successful. What worked for two of your children may not work for your third (unique) one. Non-compliance with your current techniques doesn't make a child bad—just different.

This chapter stresses two key points regarding the above definition of modification: *slight* and *environment*. (1) Slight means learning to think in moderation. Everyone needs balance—too much of anything isn't good. People who *think* in extremes believe life has to either be right or wrong, good or bad, black or white. When there isn't a middle ground, options are more limited, making modification more difficult and often impossible—setting anyone who practices extremes—up for defeat. A closer look toward the middle (the grays) and a search for compromise will make parenting more successful. (2) Environment includes, but it not limited to, how children relate to their parent's expectations. Children respond directly to their surroundings, whether good or bad. Lacking the proper parenting skills doesn't necessarily equate to disaster. Remember kids are forgiving. Your parenting techniques are not set in stone—they can be changed! Just make it happen by becoming more aware of your children's needs then acting upon them.

Most parents are already doing a good job with their kids, some might just need a tune-up to keep their children's egos running smoothly. To achieve new goals, think ahead (proactive vs. reactive) then think *behavior prevention.*

Behavior is directly affected by how a person perceives herself and her environment. If your child doesn't feel good about herself or her situation, it will be more difficult for her to *want* to behave properly.

"Why should I try anyway, my dad says I'm stupid."

Ways must be sought out to help children develop higher self-esteems. Increasing their self-esteem will encourage a higher degree of self-worth. This in turn should induce better behavior. What a wonderful cycle!

As mentioned in chapter three, *"Catch Me If You Can,"* parents must be one step ahead of the game. Catching good behavior and rewarding that *first* will be a key element. This may also include intervening before the behavior gets too far out of control. Preventing the behavior will elicit change through practicing new alternatives.

Another goal for change is giving positive reinforcement rather than negative. This point was mentioned earlier and doesn't really need to be addressed, just perhaps reiterated. We need to show our kids that life is like a half a glass of water—it's either half empty or half full. Children's attention spans are short. Therefore, when their attitudes are negative, they can easily be distracted just by moving them in a different, more positive direction. But we, too, must look at our lives the same way. The way we model behavior will be a good indication on how our children will cope with behavior.

The next goal for BM is to achieve conflict resolution. We must create harmony in the environment. I've studied parenting skills and the effects they have on children for many years yet I'm still learning with each new experience. Recently while talking to a woman about problem solving I learned how she resolved conflict between her children. She got my attention. The scenario was a familiar one: what do you do when children fight over the biggest piece or the largest glass of anything?

"She got the bigger half, that's not fair."

This woman said she would take whatever treat she was giving to her children and ask one to cut it. The catch was that the other one got first pick. This seems so simple yet so ingenious in my opinion. Splitting treats, to meet a child's specification, is almost impossible—what better and easier way to resolve this problem. The one splitting the treat will make sure he's cutting straight down the middle (that is, if he wants to protect his own interests).

It's not enough just understanding that children misbehave or cope inappropriately with their environment—alternatives must be found to change the behavior. To promote regularity in our lives, we must examine how our children grow both physically and emotionally. Maslow, a psychologist, developed a chart which he refered to as the Hierarchy of Needs. The concept supposes that people don't have the *ability* to develop unless their basic needs are met—first.

At the lowest end of the spectrum, he says that if children don't have ample food and shelter, emotional, intellectual and developmental growth will be difficult. As a result, children who experience anxiety from not feeling safe or who suffer nutritionally will have their growth impeded until these basic needs are met. Some parents might be thinking, *"Hey, my kid's safe—she has a home."*

Our children don't have the same compilation of experiences or points of reference as we do; therefore, their interpretation of the environment can be completely different than ours. As a result, they learn and grow differently than we do. The next example shows how differently a child can see things.

> One day my nephew, Charlie, was being
> tested for kindergarten.
> Examiner: "Charlie, do you know what
> season it is?"
> After a great deal of thought, he
> replied: "Yes, it's rabbit season!"

Remember, children think that there are monsters under the bed and ghosts in the closet. Their fears can seem unrealistic or over exaggerated but these are genuine fears which need to be recognized. We must consider how children are perceiving their environment and not assume because *we* know it's safe that they know it too.

This assumption reminds me of a story I recently heard in church. The setting was in the 1800s where a small child severed a main artery in her arm. Blood transfusions were rare but the doctor wanted to attempt to save her. He told the family without the transfusion the child would die. The doctor then asked the little girl's brother if he would be willing to give some blood. He hesitated for a moment but then agreed. After the transfusion was complete and the little girl was stable, the doctor turned around to find the small boy quivering on the table. The doctor asked, *"What's wrong, boy?"* His reply, *"When am I going to die?"*[1]

This small boy concluded that if he gave blood to save his sister

---

[1]Months after I heard this story, I saw a similar story in a book call Chicken Soup for the Soul. Written by Jack Canfield & Mark Victor Hansen, 1993, p. 27. I'm sure it is one in the same.

then the loss of blood means he must die. Because children don't have the same experiences or references that we do, we need to understand what exactly "*safe*" means in the minds of children. We must not assume that they feel the same as we do.

The undesirable behavior we experience with our children is due to situations where they feel threatened (backed into a corner) and they are unable to cope well. Their reaction is a direct result of the anxiety caused by their lack of control. Anxiety rears its ugly head and displays itself in a manner which we may view as 'acting out.' As we witness this display, it would be good to remember that the 'acting out' is only a small part of the big picture. Look beyond the behavior and search for the answers to what is causing the problems. Sometimes a little comfort goes a long way toward easing their anxiety—other times it may require a great deal more. The solutions are there, we may just have to look more closely for them.

In a book written by Adele Faber and Elaine Mazlish, called *"How to Talk So Kids Will Listen and Listen So Kids Will Talk,"* one of the authors says she found it helpful to physically pull out a piece of paper and write down her children's ideas in front of them so they would understand that she was really listening.

For example, her child wanted a toy from the store; she promptly wrote it down on a piece of paper. The child was calmed by this seemingly small act. As I read this concrete method of listening, it sounded so profound. All that child truly desired was to be heard (I am sure he wanted the toy too, but that wasn't what was most important). What better way to acknowledge that you are listening to your child?

Physically writing down his desires made his wishes more concrete and real in his eyes. Think about it...have you ever been in a meeting, made a suggestion and watched other members write it down? They were saying to you, *"I hear what you are saying, I like it, and your idea is important to me."* This same concept allows a child to understand that he's been heard and he can *move on.* In turn, he will feel respected (although he might not understand exactly what that means, he does understand how it feels).

Another useful remedy is listening to children and attending to their immediate needs. Often we spend more energy and time resisting our children's five-minute request. We need to determine if their requests are really so unreasonable. If the children's request is valid then we just wasted the time it would have taken to fulfill the need. I am not saying that we have to cater to their every whim but sometimes the demands for attention are just a way to seek reaffirmation that we love them unconditionally.

As mentioned in Chapter 2, *Know, "No, No"*, adults are often rushed, sometimes saying "no" more than they should. Children crave the positive which may mean tending to their immediate needs occasionally. Children test the limits to see whether or not we care. Saying "no" to their needs should always be for a good reason, not just because we say so or don't feel like dealing with them. If a pattern of continuous *acting out* is evident, perhaps we should reevaluate the situation and look at *our* behavior to see whether we are actually the ones exacerbating the problem.

On the other hand, when a parent allows undesirable behavior to continue for too long, it will be more difficult to remedy the situation. Parents often feel powerless when they can't find the answers to their problems; (sometime it truly is difficult to see the forest for the trees). Some parents are turning to *"professional"* help as a result of these inadequate feelings.

Professional help can be very good but caution should always be taken when selecting someone to evaluate your child's behavior. Professionals are people too, capable of making mistakes. Each has a *"professional opinion"* which may not apply to every child's situation. Any opinion that appears drastic should be scrutinized and not always be taken at face value. Get a second opinion.

Recently, a medication trend has risen to great and unprecedented heights. This new fad is to control our children's behavior through a medication called Ritalin. This drug is available to minimize behavioral problems for children who have Attention Deficit Disorder/Hyperactivity Disorder (ADD/ADHD).

ADD/ADHD is listed in the DSM III-R,[2] with the following symptoms. A child must meet at least eight of these criteria along with a disturbance that lasts at least six months before he is

---

[2]Judith Rappoport, M.D. and Deborah R. Ismond, M.A., Diagnositical and Statistic Manual III Training Guide for Diagnosis of Childhood Disorder Manual, 1990, p. 110.

considered affected:

◊ Often fidgets with hands or feet or squirms in seat
◊ Has difficulty remaining seated when required to do so
◊ Is easily distracted by extraneous stimuli
◊ Has difficulty awaiting turn in games or group
◊ Often blurts out answers to questions before they have been completed
◊ Has difficulty following through on instructions from others
◊ Often shifts from one uncompleted activity to another
◊ Has difficulty playing quietly
◊ Often talks excessively
◊ Often interrupts or intrudes on others
◊ Often does not seem to listen to what is being said to him or her
◊ Often loses things necessary for tasks or activities at school or at home
◊ Often engages in physically dangerous activities without considering possible consequences

I don't want to minimize the fact that there are children who *genuinely* suffer from the above problems. Children with this disorder really need medication *in conjunction with behavior modification* to combat their troubles. Yet there are many who are being grossly over-diagnosed and may only need a positive alteration within their current environment to change this so-called *"attention disorder."* I'm deeply concerned with this new propensity to *"cure our children."* Although help is essential, make sure it's the *right* help.

The craze to diagnose every child who misbehaves with Attention Deficit is cause for great concern—the statistics are staggering. I subscribe to a computer network and many teachers are reporting that 20% of their students are medicated for ADD/ADHD. It seems implausible that one out of five children can be suffering from this disease. (Unless, of course, a severe population-wide genetic mutation has occurred! If this is the case, we should consult our best environmentalist right away and start working on a hazardous waste clean-up.)

Since the mutation scenario is unlikely, we'll need to take a better look at our children's current situation or more importantly, we'll need to take a better look at our own. Maybe we are the cause of this attention problem. Are we looking for the easiest way out by blaming everything and everybody else for our children's problems?

Labeling children with this disorder holds severe consequences and should be considered carefully before any actions are taken. Medicating children is significant and should be looked at more closely. All alternatives should be exhausted before children are subject to mind alteration. Remember Electric Shock Therapy? When psychiatrists realized that the shocks minimized anxiety, they began administering it to everyone who displayed signs of depression. It worked for some yet had profound drawbacks for others, including permanent memory loss. Do we want to unnecessarily risk our children's health because it's the fastest and easiest way to deal with the problem?

Recently, my nephew was diagnosed with Post Traumatic Stress Disorder (this was after I fought with "the professionals" for three years saying that it wasn't ADD and that I did not want to medicate). The report indicated that he suffered from anxiety. I accepted the diagnosis but felt somewhat uncomfortable with the doctor's new recommendation to medicate for anxiety.

Although troubled by the recommendation, I seriously considered the medication. Many people gave their opinion—some strongly for and some strongly against medicating. Personal circumstances and time limitations didn't permit me to get the medication. I spoke with a homeopathic doctor and she recommended Chamomile (found in Chamomile tea) to reduce anxiety. I began administering the herb twice a day and have noticed some change. In addition, my nephew under-went hypnotherapy. I'm not completely convinced that the Chamomile or the hypnosis was the "cure" but psychologically, it was enough to minimize his anxiety. What I do know is that significant progress has been made without the chemicals.

My nephew is living testament—get a second, third, or fourth opinion if necessary. Be sure you are doing the right thing. I deeply respect the medical community (they are there to help) however anyone can make a mistake. Just be careful. I would caution anyone not to be too quick to accept this diagnosis. Consider the complete environment—understand the circumstances surrounding the behavior. Although pediatricians or general practitioners are invaluable—go to a mental health specialist (preferably a psychologist/psychiatrist). I would strongly recommend that a parent deals strictly with a child specialist.

Unless this is an emergency, maintain a journal indicating the problem child's behavior for a period of time before consulting a doctor. Some parents will go into the specialist describing only the child's behavior and the doctor doesn't get the complete picture. Due to the popularity of this new found disorder, some doctors might even coach a parent for the answers by saying things like:

"Does your child have difficulty with irritability?"
"Is your child having troubles listening to what you are saying?"
"Does your child have problems concentrating?"

It could be true that a child has all of these moods but it does not necessarily mean that the child has ADD. Behavior is a *symptom*, not the problem. The following are some issues that affect children either directly or *indirectly*—see whether the child is experiencing any of these concerns. Use them to fill in the journal. This will help the professionals make a more accurate diagnosis. Is your child or someone in your family experiencing a:

◊ Breakup or turmoil in a relationship
◊ Loss, stress or change in parents' job
◊ Parent/grandparent's illness
◊ Time pressures
◊ Problems with money
◊ Break in routine
◊ Birth of a new child
◊ Parent fatigue
◊ Death of a loved one
◊ Moving/changing neighborhoods, schools and friends
◊ Parent preoccupation with anything that distracts too much time from the child
◊ Parent's emotional anxiety and fears such as sadness and anger
◊ Parent who has behavioral problems such as adult ADD
◊ Loss of a pet
◊ Disappointment with their performance (school, sports, or friends)
◊ Is rest sufficient? Too little or too much
◊ Does the child have a new adult in his life?

By keeping this journal, you can supply the professional with enough information to decide whether your child really does suffer from ADD/ADHD or whether you might only need to take a CHANCE. Either way the journal can't hurt. But the improper use of medication can! Take into consideration all of the above, then create a list of issues, like the following, to take with you to the doctors.

◊ Write down the dates and times incidences occur.
◊ Is the diet consistent? Keep a log.
◊ How long has behavior persisted? Describe circumstance that created or aggravated the problem.
◊ How did the people involve react to the situation?
◊ Is the child spending too much time alone or watching television?

These things are critical with diagnosis because an overall picture is much more important than the behavior itself. Again these behaviors are the symptoms and not the problems. You may be forced to look within yourself to see whether there is anything that you are doing that is affecting the behavior.

Parent Behavior—>Child Reaction

Children react to their environment and any type of *stressor* can cause them to react adversely. If you have lost your job, that stress will be transposed onto your children. If you think about it, doesn't it seem as though your kids always act up when you are having a crummy day? It's possible that they are reacting to your anxiety. If you are the one who has the anxiety then you are the one who needs the chill pill—not them.

"I really mean it this time!"

Another area where children react is when you continually threaten them with *next time.* We are all guilty of this, including myself. I try to be consistent, but I see myself caving in. I start thinking,

> *"Oh, I was too harsh...I am not mad anymore...I will give him a break—this time—but this is the last time! I swear."*

This is probably one of the worst things we can do. By stating that you really mean it *this* time, you are saying that you didn't mean it the other five times you said it. As mentioned earlier, children learn from experience. If experience tells them that it will take five times until you mean it, they will not listen until you say it the fifth time. I learned this the hard way and I find that it's a difficult habit to break. It feels uncomfortable for everyone when a change needs to occur. If you are guilty of the "next time" practice, there's still time to redeem yourself—just do it!

Behavior modification is essential to promoting regularity. Take time to evaluate yourself and your children. Many of your interactive problems may just need a small adjustment. Your children depend on you for all the "right" answers. Make sure the decisions you make are done with a full conscience!

Behavior modification takes time. Look hard at your life and decide how you really want to guide your children. They grow up so quickly, make sure you spend your time with them wisely. *Here's your CHANCE*, make it count! Good luck and good parenting.

Homework

BM Helps Regularity

Think about some of the behavioral problems that you want to change and write them down. It might be best to start with something easy, like not running through the house. Initially, you will need to dedicate a great deal of time to each change—simply because these new practices are foreign to you and your child. Time, consistency and focus will be needed to accomplish these goals. Move forward only when you feel comfortable that the changes have occurred.

1.   5.
2.   6.
3.   7.
4.   8.

Now write down all the activities that your child enjoys. Some examples may be movies, roasting marshmallows, or going to the zoo.

1.   5.
2.   6.
3.   7.
4.   8.

Use the second list as ideas for rewarding your kids. Your children want and need to have quality time with you. Remember too that the bad behavior may just be their way of telling you that they need you to see them. In the journal, track your progress. Good luck.

Journal Notes

Conclusion

One day I noticed an army of ants building a mound on the sidewalk near my home. I watched them as they all worked building this tremendously large structure...one grain of sand at a time. These small insects were so fascinating.

The next day, out of curiosity, I checked their progress. As I approached the area, I found the mound completely destroyed—demolished by a lawn mower. Half of the ants were dead on the walk, the other half were diligently picking up their dead and rebuilding the mound—ironically in the exact same spot where they were the day before. I admired their hard work from the day before; yet, I was confused as to why they stayed in an area which was *obviously* destructive.

I see an instructive analogy for us parents in the futile ant-work. We continue using the same parenting methods over and over again, often yielding the same unsuccessful results. But we neglect to see the *obvious*—that the techniques don't work.

Due to time constraints and the demands of every day responsibilities. We focus getting through the here and now; thereby creating urgency and making parenting goals more short-term, immediate and limited. The time and energy required to meet these long-term goals becomes restricted.

Although, we have a great desire to be the best parents that we can be—to build that mound of hope and make a difference—we catch ourselves in a rut. Our brain is filled with cobwebs and the solutions do not come easily—we feel defeated. The results are parental burn-out and distress. We are constantly picking up and rebuilding one grain of sand at a time. Often it feels as though our efforts are in vain. But if we just change our strategies we can change our circumstances. Let us work smarter, not harder.

Take a CHANCE—Dare to be Different

What we need to do is find a new positive place to build our mound, to try new techniques, and to venture out away from the lawn mower. But, to do this, we must be willing to change.

Changing how we *view* our children has been the goal of this book. We need to give our kids a CHANCE to learn and grow in the best possible environment that we can provide them. We must help them develop a positive self image in order that they will truly love themselves and the world around them.

I would like to leave you with two thoughts, the first from some notes I took in college, the second written by James Baldwin:

****

Teach a child high standards and s/he will strive toward excellence.

"Children have never been very good at listening to their elders—But they have never failed to imitate them."

****

INDEX

ORDER FORM

Name _____

Address _____

_____

Telephone Number ( )_____

Quantity   @Price   Shipping & Handling   Total

_____ $14.95 each   +$3.00 per book   =   _____

Send check or money order to:

Christina Dalpiaz
P.O. Box 371815
Denver, CO 80237-1815

For more information on CHANCE call:
(303)696-SAFE

Journal Notes

Journal Notes

Journal Notes

Journal Notes

Journal Notes

Journal Notes